The Geffrye Almshouses

Researched and written in the
Greater London Council Historic Buildings Division
by Neil Burton.

Price £2.50 excluding postage

© Geffrye Museum 1979

Published for the Geffrye Museum
by the Inner London Education Authority

ISBN 0 7085 0036 6

Contents

Acknowledgements

The water-colour on the front cover is reproduced by kind permission of the Worshipful Company of Ironmongers; the portrait of Sir Robert Geffrye on page 43 by kind permission of the Governors of Bridewell Hospital. In addition, the author would like to thank Mr A F Kelsall of the Greater London Council Historic Buildings Division for permission to incorporate the results of his research on Shoreditch almshouses and for many helpful comments.

Preface

The buildings which house the Geffrye Museum have always constituted one of its most attractive features, and much work has been undertaken over the past decade or so to ensure that what little remains of the original interior is not only respected but restored as convincingly as possible. The chapel, built originally as a 'Great Room' for official functions, but within two years adapted for worship and enlarged later, probably in 1791, has now been restored to its original appearance, and the splendid Baroque memorial to Sir Robert Geffrye, for which Richard Saunders was paid £85 in 1704, has been returned to the place which it occupied between 1883 and 1911. One of the original staircases survives in the South Wing, as well as two rooms which give an idea of the internal arrangement of the building during the 200 years in which it fulfilled its function as almshouses.

Almost nothing of old Shoreditch survives, apart from St Leonard's Church (by George Dance the Elder), and it is nearly impossible to visualise its appearance in the early 18th century when it contained no fewer than nineteen almshouses, all founded by private charity. One of the most valuable aspects of this book is that it sets the Geffrye Almshouses in their socio-historical context, demonstrating both how it resembled and differed from other comparable foundations in the last years of the 17th century and the early part of the 18th. It tells a fascinating story, based on contemporary documents in the archives of the Ironmongers' Company, which have never been previously studied in depth, and whose study has revealed how the building actually functioned and even something of the lives of its occupants.

That this book has come to be written is mainly due to the Greater London Council's Surveyor of Historic Buildings, Mr B Ashley Barker who, taking up a remark of mine that someone should write the history of this building, promptly made one of his team of historians available to undertake the work, which I was only too pleased to commission on behalf of the museum. I trust that he is as pleased with the result as I am.

Jeffery Daniels
Director

Chapter one

The foundation
of the almshouses

Sir Robert Geffrye

Robert Geffrye came from Cornwall. He was born in 1613 in the parish of Landrake, which lies at the eastern edge of the county next to the estuary of the river Lynher, and was baptised in the church there on 24 May of that year. His family was neither long-established nor wealthy. Fragments of information contained in wills and deeds suggest that his father may have come to Landrake at the beginning of the seventeenth century, perhaps from Truro. Robert Geffrye the elder was probably a yeoman or small farmer, for in 1670 the only one of his sons to remain in Cornwall is mentioned as the tenant of a small-holding of twenty-three acres. Some of the female members of the family married in the district, but the name of Geffrye only survived in Landrake for two generations and died with Zenobia Geffrye in 1673[1].

When he was fifteen or sixteen the younger Robert left Cornwall and came to London, which was already undergoing that process of rapid commercial expansion which eventually made it the largest town and most important business centre in the world. The prospects of wealth and improved social status which were offered to young provincials attracted many of them to the capital; a large number, if not actually the majority, of the great merchants and traders in the City during the seventeenth century had been born and brought up outside London. At the time of Robert's arrival, most London trade was under the control of the various companies, which were the descendants of the medieval trade guilds, and it was almost essential for any would-be trader to obtain membership of one of them. The commonest method of entry was by serving a seven year period of apprenticeship with someone who was already a freeman. Geffrye was bound apprentice to a Mr Richard Peate and in 1637 he was admitted to the freedom of the Ironmongers' Company[2].

By this date it was not essential for a freeman to pursue the trade or craft of the company to which he belonged and there is nothing which suggests that Geffrye had anything to do with ironmongery. His early career in London remains a mystery, but by the 1650s he had become a merchant with interests in India and the Far East and he was one of the many who petitioned Parliament, in 1654, against giving the monopoly over trade in these areas to the East India Company. Africa was another of his theatres of operation. When the Royal Africa Company was re-founded in 1670, Geffrye was among the original shareholders and his connection with the company was continued at least until 1691, when he was elected a member of the Court of Assistants, the governing body. Most of the profits of the Royal Africa Company came from the trade in black slaves and part of the wealth which was eventually used to build the Geffrye almshouses may have been derived from this unhappy source.

A good deal of confusion has arisen concerning Robert Geffrye's business interests because there were at least three merchants of this name in London after the Commonwealth. Undoubtedly the richest was John Jeffery, a successful adventurer in the Virginia tobacco trade, who also had interests in Russia and Sweden. It was he, and not Robert, who lost ten thousand pounds worth of tobacco in the Great Fire and was subsequently nicknamed 'The Great Smoker'. After his death in 1688 his business was carried on by his nephew Jeffery Jeffery, and to complicate the issue still further both the older men were friends and political adherents of George Jefferies, later Lord Chief Justice, who conducted the infamous 'Bloody Assizes' in the west of England after Monmouth's rebellion. None of these men spelt his name in a consistent way and Robert Geffrye appears at various times as Jeffrye, Jeffery, Geffery and Geffrye. The last is the spelling in the will which established the almshouses and it is employed throughout this book.

At some time during the Commonwealth, Geffrye was elected to the Livery of the Ironmongers' Company. All the City companies were organised in roughly the same way and consisted of the Freemen, numbering anything up to fifty or sixty in the larger companies, and an inner circle called the Livery, from which the positions of the chief officers were filled annually by election. In the Ironmongers' Company the officers were the Master and the Senior and Junior Wardens. Having joined the Livery, a man might reasonably expect to hold all of these offices if he lived long enough, though many preferred to pay a substantial cash fine in order to be excused the time-consuming duties. The first distinction which Geffrye enjoyed was to be chosen as the representative of the Ironmongers at the entertainment given by all the City companies together in 1660, to welcome Charles II back to the throne. The choice reflected Geffrye's political convictions which were strongly Royalist and remained so for the whole of his life. In 1664 he was elected Warden and, in 1667, Master of his company; having served the required year in the latter post he was discharged of further obligation. Geffrye then turned from company administration to a wider field. He had been elected a Deputy Alderman in 1663; this junior post in the hierarchy of the government of the City provided the entrée to a more influential and lucrative world.

The twenty years after 1668 were a turbulent passage in the relations between the Crown and the City, as first Charles II and then his brother James attempted to gain control of London's great financial resources and to subvert those institutions which would not submit to being controlled. Geffrye, with his Royalist sympathies, was well-placed to benefit by the intervention of the Court. In October 1673 he received a Knighthood, for reasons which are not at all clear, perhaps for special services to the King. Two years later he held the office of Sheriff of London, which was of considerable importance, since the Sheriff was responsible for selecting the juries for hearings in the City Courts; immediately after relinquishing this office he was elected a member of the Court of Aldermen, the governing body of the City, as representative of Cordwainer ward. Further advancement followed. In 1681 the King removed several of the officers commanding the City trained bands, or militia, whose loyalty was suspect and Geffrye was one of those put in their stead. During the period that the Charter of the City was suspended and the elective process replaced by a Royal Commission under 'Quo Warranto' proceedings, Geffrye was not only confirmed in his appointment as Alderman but, in 1685, was declared Lord Mayor of London by royal fiat and Master of the Ironmongers' Company for a second time. He proved just as loyal to James II and it was only when faced with the desire of the King to repeal the Test Act, thereby admitting Roman Catholics and Dissenters into public office and giving them freedom of worship, that Geffrye abandoned the Court party. In 1687 he asked to be released from the office of Alderman, because he could no longer support the policy of the Crown.

After the accession of Mary and William of Orange in 1688, Geffrye resumed his post as Alderman of Cordwainer under the restored City Charter and held it for the rest of his lifetime, but the new political climate was not in his interest. William and Mary naturally favoured the Whigs. The adherents of the Stuarts were discredited and the priviliges of institutions like the Royal Africa Company, which had been under the protection of King James, were eroded. Henceforward Geffrye, who was by now seventy-five years old, played little part in City politics. His wife Priscilla had died childless in 1676, at their house in Lime Street, and he had no close family[3]. For the remaining fifteen years of his life he seems to have turned his attention from trade and politics to matters of charity. As an Alderman he was already concerned with the financing and administration of the great charitable institutions which were the City's responsibility. In the late seventeenth century there were five major institutions of this kind in London: the hospitals of St Bartholomew, St Thomas, Christ, Bethlehem and Bridewell. Although many of the decisions affecting the hospitals were taken by the Court of Aldermen, each had its own president who had more particular responsibility. In 1689 Geffrye offered himself as President of Bethlehem and Bridewell Hospitals and was elected. In February 1691/2 he applied for the presidency of St Thomas's, but was turned down in favour of his city colleague Sir Robert Clayton. In 1692 he was re-elected President of the two hospitals and he continued to hold office until his death in 1704. There are legends concerning the disciplinary floggings ordered by Sir Robert at Bridewell, where prostitutes were punished, but this was a time of harsh punishments and he may not have been unusually cruel. He was certainly generous to Bethlehem and Bridewell in his will, in which he not only gave substantial sums of money to both these hospitals, but also established a third to supplement them.

Charity in England in the Seventeenth and Eighteenth centuries

Before looking at the bequests of Sir Robert Geffrye in detail it may be helpful to survey briefly some of the more important characteristics of English private charity in the period preceding his death. The sick, poor, old and unfortunate of medieval England were cared for chiefly by the church and it has been estimated that there were over seven hundred institutions devoted to this work at the beginning of the sixteenth century. The money to support the hospitals was largely obtained from charitable gifts, since the Roman Catholic religion taught that donations of this kind, made to the church, earned remission for the soul in Purgatory.

King Henry VIII's Reformation of the church abolished most of the communities which had been responsible for running the various hospitals. In London, the two great foundations of St Thomas and St Bartholomew were given into the hands of the civil authorities and continued to function, but many others ceased to exist. Some years later King Edward VI founded several new hospitals in London to deal with specific classes of unfortunates: Christ's Hospital for orphans and poor men's children, Bethlehem Hospital (or Bedlam) for the insane and Bridewell Hospital for the 'idle and vicious', particularly prostitutes. The new hospitals were placed on the same footing as the other establishments and given buildings and endowments, but they could not hope to cater for all the poor in London; both in the capital and in the provinces large number of helpless people remained uncared for.

From the middle of the sixteenth century onward an increasing amount of private wealth was given for the assistance of the poor and, again, this was partly a result of religious pressure. The reformed religion held that it was the responsibility of each individual to care for his fellows in need. Within a generation of the dissolution of the monasteries their contribution to English charity had been at least partly made up by private benefactors, although gifts now went directly to charity and not through the medium of a religious foundation. By 1600 it was generally expected that every prosperous Englishman would leave a portion of his wealth to charity when he died and failure to do so was regarded as remiss. The amount of money given in this way was staggeringly large. W K Jordan's analysis of the wills proved in only ten of the English counties, between 1490 and 1660, produced a total sum of £3,102,696 9s 0d given for charitable purposes in this period[4]. As always, it is important to treat these figures with caution, but the total sum is undeniably impressive and Jordan's study establishes beyond doubt that the care of the poor and needy became a major social preoccupation in England after about 1550.

The principal donors in the medieval period had been the nobility and, to a lesser extent, the gentry; the principal donors in the seventeenth and eighteenth centuries came from the middle class. Of all the various sub-sections of this class merchants were by far the most generous, especially the merchants of the City of London. A large proportion of the many vast mercantile fortunes made in the City was laid out in setting up charities of all kinds. Nearly sixty-one percent of

Jordan's total, £1,889,211 12s in all, was given by the inhabitants of London and Middlesex for charitable purposes[5]. The benefits were not confined to the place in which the donor lived, and many merchants who had left their rural origins for the City used some of their wealth to benefit the parish or village from which they had come.

The rate of giving was not constant, but fluctuated in response to social pressures. In the two centuries after 1550, the thirty years after 1610 and the forty years after 1700 stand out as periods of conspicuous generosity. According to Jordan, the amount of money given during the first period eclipsed anything before it; subsequent research suggests that the real value of these charitable donations may not have been so great as was previously thought, but it was still greater than the total for the previous sixty years. The increase in charitable benefactions after 1610 was a direct result of the enactment of the Statute of Charitable Uses in 1601, which regularised the administration of charitable trusts. Although some charitable donations were given directly, the majority were left in perpetual trust. From the thirteenth century onwards, gifts and bequests for such purposes had been placed under the trusteeship of religious orders and complaints about the administration of the trusts were heard in the ecclesiastical courts. During the fifteenth century the Court of Chancery gradually took over the responsibility for the supervision of charitable trusts from the church courts, but the law relating to them remained without any established practice and was open to considerable dispute. The Statute of Charitable Uses codified the principal laws relating to trusts: its preamble listed a wide variety of purposes that were to be considered charitable and offered them favourable treatment. In the course of time this preamble, of which the relevant portion is given here, became the classic statement of charitable purposes:

'For the relief of aged, impotent and poor people, some for the maintenance of soldiers and mariners, schools of learning, free schools and scholars in universities, some for repair of bridges, ports, havens, causeways, churches, sea-banks and highways, some for education and payment of orphans, some for or towards relief, stock or maintenance for houses of correction, some for marriages of poor maids, some for supportation aid and help young tradesmen, handicraftsmen and persons decayed; and others for relief or redemptions of prisoners and captives and for aid or ease of any poor inhabitant concerning payment of fifteens, setting out of soldiers and other taxes.'

By the terms of the statute, charitable trusts were given several important privileges; they were exempted from the role against perpetuities, they were to be considered 'good' in law, even if the terms of the bequest establishing the trust were imprecise. Also, by the custom known as *cy-pres*, if the original purpose of the trust should fail, the Lord Chancellor could specify a new one as near as possible to the original intention of the donor. The statute also made provision for the investigation of abuses of trust funds. Such privileges and safeguards gave an incentive to all charitable persons, who could now be reasonably certain that their gifts would not be diverted to pay for interminable law-suits or find their way into the pockets of their trustees. The great increase in the flow of charitable donations after 1610 was, without doubt, a direct consequence of the greater security offered by this statute.

During the Civil War and the Commonwealth, the total amount of money given for charity was much less than in the previous decades. Finance was required for more immediate purposes and there can have been little inducement to set up new charitable trusts in such troubled times. The reigns of Charles II and James II were also unfavourable for charitable donors; both the later Stuarts made heavy demands on the financial resources of the City of London and did nothing to encourage the generosity of the merchant community. After the Revolution of 1688, however, the volume of charitable bequests began to increase once more. Taking charities for the aged as an example, the number of new almshouse foundations in the period 1696 to 1745 totalled one hundred and sixteen, only five less than the total for 1596 to 1646, while bequests for the benefit of non-residential charities were nearly double those of the earlier period[6]. The increase was partly a consequence of the greater social and institutional stability of the years after 1688, which encouraged gifts made for the benefit of posterity, but it was greatly stimulated by new developments in financial organisation.

Before the 1690s, many charitable bequests had been given singly, each charitable object being financed by one donor. A rich donor might establish an almshouse or a school, paying for the site and buildings and also providing an endowment to ensure an income for the maintenance of the charity; a donor with less money at his disposal might endow a dole which would provide an occasional distribution of money or food to a limited number of deserving poor. There was no very satisfactory method by which several donors could combine together in one undertaking over a number of years. Any sum could, of course, be given to one of the great charitable institutions, such as one of the hospitals in London, but money given in this way purchased no influence on policy and was absorbed into the current account, with nothing to perpetuate the name of the donor. The rapid increase in the number of businesses in the City after 1690 which were organised on joint-stock principles had a marked effect on the pattern of charitable giving. The new commercial methods were applied to the raising of money for good works and several charitable societies were formed which opened subscription lists, similar to the lists of shareholders of individual companies. By 1700 the Society for the Propagation of Christian Knowledge and the Society for the Reformation of Manners, which both drew their income entirely from subscriptions, were firmly established. Many people were pleased to pledge a small annual subscription for a worthy purpose and considerable sums were raised in this way, far surpassing even the most generous individual bequests.

The new societies usually concentrated their efforts on providing education, which was as much the favourite charity of the eighteenth century as almshouses were of the seventeenth, but some of the older institutions quickly realised the advantages of subscription lists. In particular the hospitals, which had always been dependent upon a steady flow of bequests to defray their running costs, were attracted by the size and regularity of income obtained in this way. St Bartholomew's, for example, raised £40,000 by subscription between 1720 and 1748. Almshouses did not lend themselves so readily to the modern method of financing, partly because they had no need of it, being static foundations whose financial needs, after the buildings had been completed, were small and regular. The pensions of the almspeople, the salaries of the officers and the cost of maintaining the buildings were the only outgoings, and these were often covered by the income of the founding trust.

The popularity of subscription charities was so great that an increasing amount of money was diverted away from older forms. Another factor was that the equilibrium of almshouse foundations did not appeal to the majority of eighteenth century donors, who preferred to give their money to dynamic organisations, committed to the improvement of society through education or medicine. As a result, the number of new residential charities for the elderly declined after about 1735. Fresh impetus was given to almshouse foundations by the Industrial Revolution, which threw up as many large private fortunes as the commercial expansion of the seventeenth century and a number of new foundations were made in the period 1800-1850. Many older almshouses were re-founded or re-built with money from the same sources. In the parish of Shoreditch, for example, there were four new foundations and three re-foundations during these fifty years. After the mid century, new developments in philanthrophy once again relegated almshouses to a relatively unimportant place.

The Ironmongers' Company and Sir Robert Geffrye's will

One of the problems confronting any person wishing to set up a charity was the difficulty of finding dependable trustees, who would not only look after their trust honestly, without diverting too much money for dubious purposes, but would also appoint worthy successors. When a bequest was made for the benefit of a specific parish, the members of the vestry were very often chosen as trustees. Before the introduction of more modern forms of local government, the vestries were responsible for the carrying out of most necessary services in the parish, including the care of the poor; they were elected and perpetual. Charities with a wider scope required trustees without such particular interests and, for the majority of merchant donors, a satisfactory solution was found by employing one of the City Livery Companies as trustee.

In most cases the original function of the companies as trade guilds, enforcing standards of craftsmanship, had withered away, but they continued to exercise control over much of the business conducted in the City. It was almost impossible for a merchant to trade in London without belonging to one of the companies. The machinery of government was also in their hands. Until 1742, the Lord Mayor was always chosen from the membership of the twelve leading companies and the holders of the lesser offices of Sheriff and Alderman were customarily drawn from both the great and the much larger number of smaller companies. In some respects they were similar to the gentlemen's clubs of the nineteenth century, providing a social bond between the members as well as a means of entry into the hierarchy of government. The income of each company was derived partly from fines levied on admission to the status of freeman, or for refusing to serve in one of the elected offices and, increasingly in the sixteenth and seventeenth centuries, from the bequests made by charitable donors in recognition of the company's services as trustee.

By the beginning of the eighteenth century all the major companies had been in existence for several hundred years; the Ironmongers' Company, for example, received its charter of incorporation in 1464 and is mentioned over two-hundred years earlier in proclamations of the late twelfth century. This apparent permanence, taken together with a membership composed mainly of traders accustomed to handling large sums of money, made the companies ideal trustees for charitable bequests; from the mid-fifteenth century onwards, an increasing number of such trusts were placed under the control of the company courts. The companies themselves were eager to accept the responsibility. In most cases the trusts made some provision specifically for the benefit of their members, either for 'poor decayed freemen' or for apprentices needing a loan to set up in business. There was an incidental financial advantage to be gained from administering a large capital sum, as the founder of the trust often made a direct reward to the company in anticipation of its services. In several cases, the income obtained from fines by the smaller companies was insufficient and their survival into the eighteenth century was only made possible by the income from charitable trusts. Even the larger companies drew a very substantial part of their revenue from charitable endowments.

The number of trusts given into the care of the London companies declined sharply after 1688, as the subscription charities gained in popularity. But during the eighteenth and, more especially, during the nineteenth century, the value of the trusts in company care steadily increased. Much trust money was invested in land, either in the City itself or in the suburbs; as the population of the capital increased and more ground was required for housing and industrial purposes, such land could command higher and higher prices. By the 1850s land in Central London had become so valuable that many companies chose to sell up and use the money to re-establish their charities in the country. The change in the value of charity land is illustrated by the Geffrye almshouse site in the Kingsland Road, which was purchased in 1712 for £200 and sold in 1910 for £24,000.

Sir Robert Geffrye's will[7], which was proved in 1704, is in many ways a perfect illustration of the forms of charity which were most popular in the preceding century. Geffrye had a substantial, though not enormous, fortune amounting altogether to about £13,000; he had no direct heirs and there was apparently no one else whom he regarded as a substitute. His will is generous to such members of his family as are mentioned, the children of his neice Rebecca Scroton and his sister Catherine, but the bulk of his estate was left to charity.

Bridewell and Bethlehem each received direct gifts of £400 from their recent president 'towards the relief of poor harboured within these hospitals' and Christ's Hospital, St Thomas's and St Bartholomew's were given £200 apiece. Sir Robert's loyalty to the established church was underlined by the gift of £10 to each of thirty poor ministers' widows and he also gave £50 to the church-wardens of his own parish of St Dionis Backchurch 'towards payment of the just debts of the said parish'. These were all outright gifts, but the remainder of the estate was left in the form of several trusts to be administered by the Iron-mongers' Company. The sum of £400 was to be used for the purchase of property in or near London and the rents and profits derived from the property were to form 'an allowance to some person to read Divine service in the parish of St Dionis Backchurch twice every day in the week except Sundays'. If only three days elapsed without a service the money was to revert to Bridewell and Bethlehem hospitals. A further sum of £520 was to be invested in a similar way, to provide two shillings a week for bread for the poor inhabitants of Landrake in Cornwall; the profits remaining after this dole had been paid were to be used to provide a schoolmaster to instruct the children of Landrake in reading, writing and the catechism. For their trouble in administering these two chari-ties, the Ironmongers' were given £200 and a pair of silver flagons, which are still in the Company's possession.

The executors of the will were Catherine Geffrye, Sir William Russell, Sir Gabriel Roberts and Sir William Gore, all of whom were either distant relations or business associates. They were charged with carrying out the bequests of the will and were also instructed to have a monument made for Sir Robert and his wife to be put up in St Dionis for a total cost of £80. The executors commis-sioned a carver named Saunders to make the monument, for which he was ultimately paid £85[8]. This was almost certainly Richard Saunders, a wood carver, whose best-known works were the statues of Gog and Magog which stood in the Guildhall until they were destroyed in the Second World War. He worked mainly for the City companies and it was probably for this reason that he was employed by the executors. The monument, which is now in the almshouse chapel, is a very competent piece which shows that Saunders had considerable skill in carving marble as well as wood. In Hatton's 'New View of London' it was described as 'a very spacious and beautiful white and veined polished marble monument adorned with the sword and mace in saltier and the cap of maintenance done in Basso Relievo at the lower end of the monument; also with cherubims, urns, festoons, Death's heads and, between two cupids weeping, his arms and (the) inscription appearing within a curious mantling, carved round and gilt in imitation of a frieze'.

All the estate remaining, after these specific payments had been made, was to be converted into cash by the executors and paid over to the Ironmongers' Company 'that they shall and do by and with the consent and advice of my executors . . . with part of the income received by my executors pur-chase a convenient piece of ground, in or near to the City of London whereon to erect and build an Almshouse for so many poor people as the monies arising by the residuary part of my estate (after the rate of six pounds per annum each person and fifteen shillings a piece yearly for gowns) may extend or amount unto.' After the purchase of the site, the residue was to be laid out, like the other trust funds, in the purchase of land and buildings in or near London. The profits from these investments were to be used to pay for building the almshouses, to supply any funds necessary for maintenance and repair and to provide the annual pensions for the inhabitants.

Despite its undoubted generosity, the loose way in which the will was drawn up was to delay the carrying out of its main purpose. The two major stumblingblocks were the obligation imposed on the trustees to obtain the agreement of the executors to any course of action and the fact that the charity was to be extended to as many poor people as possible and not a finite number. At first all went smoothly. The Company established a small committee to deal with all matters relating to the trusts and authorised it to negotiate with the executors, although all major decisions of policy or finance were to be referred back to the full Court of the Company. This committee, which was usually known as the Geffrye's Charity Committee, remained in existence for the whole life of the almshouses in London and was the governing body responsible for routine supervision, only invoking the full Court on major matters of policy[9]. In July 1704 the first instalment of £4,000 was paid over to the Committee, whose members at once began to inspect various London properties with a view to purchase. The executors estimated that there would be about another £5,000 forthcoming from the estate and it was thought that the total would be more than adequate for the purposes of the charitable trusts. The Committee hoped to avoid being at the expense of purchasing ground for the almshouse building itself, because the Company already owned a quantity of land in London, part of which might be suitable. By May 1705 the Committee had settled on a piece of company land near Moorfields and, with the verbal approval of one of the executors, had gone so far as to buy out the sitting tenants. But the rest of the executors now objected to the proposal and, at a meeting held on the 9 August 1705, 'both Sir William Gore and Sir Gabriel Roberts declared with some vehemency their utter dislike of the company's ground to build Sir Robert Geffrye's Almshouses on.' The principal reason for their objecting was that they did not consider the land public enough; it did not front on to a main road and Sir Robert's generosity would not be decently advertised. Instead, the executors suggested that a suitable piece of ground with good public frontage might be had in Shoreditch or Bethnal Green.

To resolve this dispute, the Company resorted to the courts and brought a bill in equity against the executors. The suit was delayed by the death of Sir Gabriel Roberts and was not heard until February 1707[10]. The complaint of the Company rehearses the difficulties of the almshouse trust, mentioning the dispute over a suitable site and another dispute about whether the Company could build the almshouses with money from the capital sum handed over by the executors or whether, as the executors maintained, the cost of building would have to be paid out of the rents and profits from investments. The matter was referred to Mr Keck, one of the Masters in Chancery, to prepare a report which was duly presented in July 1708. In sum, the findings of the Master supported the executors in all the main points. He directed that a piece of land be purchased out of the capital sum, within ten miles of London and that the buildings were to be erected out of the interest obtained on the remainder. He further ordered that 'as a proper ornament to such building a handsome effigie of the founder is to be erected in the front or other convenient and proper place.' All the costs of the legal action were to be paid out of the charity estate.

The Company did not find another site easy to come by. In November 1711 the Clerk of the Company wrote to John Roberts at Landrake:

'It is scarce credible to think how difficult it is to procure a proper piece of freehold ground both publicke and near the Cittye.'

Nothing suitable could be found by private enquiry and, in the end, it was found necessary to place an advertisement in *The Postman* in the following words:

'If any person hath an acre of freehold ground, little more or less to sell fronting any the roads leading from London to Hackney, Islington, Mile End or Kingsland (either coachway or footway) let him repair to Mr Morris at Ironmongers' Hall in Fenchurch Street who will treat for the purchase thereof.'

The advertisement appeared in November 1711 and by March of the following year the Committee had agreed to purchase a plot belonging to Mr Hunt, with a frontage of about three hundred and ninety feet towards the Kingsland Road and a depth of one hundred and eighty. The sale was completed on 26 March 1712 after payment of the purchase price of £200[12].

Shoreditch at the time of the foundation

The parish of St Leonard's Shoreditch was one of the first areas bordering the City of London to be built up to any considerable extent. In 1415 the Lord Mayor of London 'caused the walls of the City to be broken towards Moorfields and built the postern called Moorgate, for the ease of the citizens to walk that way upon causeways towards Islington and Hoxton'. This must have made the south west of Shoreditch more accessible from the City; the south east already had excellent communications by way of Bishopsgate and what is now Shoreditch High Street. During the sixteenth and seventeenth centuries the population of Shoreditch steadily increased and the district became relatively fashionable, especially among foreign envoys. The Portuguese Ambassador was living in Hoxton Street in 1568 and a Venetian called Jerome Bassano bought himself a considerable house there in 1590. But at the beginning of the eighteenth century Shoreditch was still a suburban parish. The southern portion, from the City boundary as far north as Worship Street, was densely built-up and the edges of the major roads, Church Street, Hoxton Street and the road to Ware were dotted with houses, but the land between them was open ground.

Hoxton was a village in its own right, well-known for The Curtain and other theatres, for its pleasure gardens and for its nurseries and market gardens. The two residential squares which were begun at the southern edge of Hoxton in the late seventeenth century bear witness to its continued attraction as a place of residence for the well-to-do. Daniel Defoe was brought up just outside the parish in the mid-seventeenth century and in 1725 he wrote with amazement at the development of this area:

'To come to the North Side of the Town, and beginning at Shoreditch, West, and Hoxton Square, and Charles Square adjoining, and the streets intended for a Market-Place, those were all open fields from Aniseed clear' (St Agnes-le-Claire—another name for the eastward continuation of Old Street) 'To Hoxton Town, till the year 1689 or thereabouts; Pitfield Street was a Bank, parting two Pasture Grounds, and Ask's Hospital was another field.'[13]

Hoxton seems to have become less popular after about 1700 and Charles Square and Hoxton Square were left uncompleted for over half a century. There was increasing competition from new estates in other parts of Middlesex, including Spitalfields on the eastern side of the City and Holborn and Bloomsbury to the north, besides a number of others between London and Westminster. Hoxton could not compete with these newer and more fashionable developments.

North of Hoxton was open fields; to the east was the road to Ware, now called the Kingsland Road. In 1602 John Stow commented that this road was, 'built upon either side more than a good flight shot, towards Kingsland, Newington, Totanham, etc.' One hundred years later, things had changed very little and the houses still stretched only as far north as the present Waterson Street. Between the Kingsland Road and Hoxton Street the unbuilt land was occupied by a large number of nurseries and market gardens. The district was widely-known for the excellence of these gardens, which continued in existence until the middle of the eighteenth century. One of the proprietors was Thomas Fairchild, author of *The City Gardener* published in 1722, which can fairly claim to be the pioneer English work on practical gardening. On Chassereau's map of Shoreditch, made in 1745, the gardens with their small plots show up in obvious contrast to the more open agricultural land lying east of the Kingsland Road. Here the fields stretched without a break to the boundary with Hackney and Bethnal Green. Almost every field contained a pond, a reminder that the land was low-lying and, in places, marshy.

In the Middle Ages the nuns of Holywell Priory must have dispensed charity to Shoreditch, but the first almshouse to be built after the Reformation was Fuller's Hospital in Old Street, which was erected between 1592 and 1605; Walter's, Watson's, Lady Lumley's and the Dutch Almshouses all followed at intervals during the seventeenth century, but none of these were as grand as Robert Aske's Hospital, erected in Pitfield Street in 1695 to the design of Robert Hooke, friend of Sir Christopher Wren and architect of Bethlehem Hospital. Twenty poor single freemen of the Haberdashers' Company and twenty sons of freemen were accommodated in a large and splendid building. It must have provided an inducement for other charities because, in the two decades after

1695, another five almshouses were built in the district, including Sir Robert Geffrye's.

Shoreditch can probably boast more almshouse foundations than any other parish in Middlesex and the parishes on the eastern side of the City were by far the most popular location for institutions of this kind. Some of the reasons for this popularity are obvious. From the point of view of the City Companies, who acted as trustees for a very large proportion of the charitable trusts of the London area, the eastern parishes had the great advantage of being near the company halls and more convenient of access than the parishes to the north and west, or those across the river to the south. Almshouses in the eastern parishes were easier to supervise and abuses of the trusts were less likely to occur. The almspeople themselves were probably pleased to be able to walk the short distance into London, either to see their friends or to work there. This must have been essential for some pensioners. Although the inhabitants of the Geffrye almshouses were given a sufficient pension to pay for food and clothing, many of the other foundations were less generous or less well-endowed and their inmates would have had to supplement their regular allowance with an earned income.

A less obvious factor in the selection of an almshouse site is the availability of land. Much of the land on the edge of London was owned by a small number of wealthy titled landlords, who were often reluctant to sell off land for piecemeal building, especially when they could make a greater profit by leasing large amounts of land for estate development. But the eastern parishes were already broken up into a large number of freeholds, many of them small in area. Charity trustees always preferred to purchase freehold land for their buildings; very often they were explicitly instructed to do so by the donor. They were seldom in a position to purchase more than a small amount of land at any one time. It is not possible to say with any certainty whether the cost of land in Shoreditch and Stepney was higher or lower than in other parishes at the same distance from London, although the difficulty which the Ironmongers' encountered in trying to locate a suitable piece of ground for their almshouse suggests that the market in these areas may have been starved, which would tend to increase the price. Their failure might equally well have been caused by the lack of sites with a suitable frontage and the land which they ultimately bought does not seem to have been unduly expensive.

Chapter two

The building
of the almshouses

The design of the building and the designers

As soon as the purchase of the ground had been completed the Committee turned to the business of building which had now been delayed for six years, but the omens for building were not good. Only a fortnight after completion, the Company became aware that Parliament was discussing the possibility of imposing a tax on all bricks and lime used for building in London and its suburbs. Such a tax would greatly increase the cost of the almshouses and it was ultimately decided that the members of the Committee should petition Parliament to have them exempted from the Bill. Their petition was presented with others in the same vein on the 21 April 1712 and it was entirely successful; a week later, both bricks and lime were struck out from the Bill and stamped vellum, parchment and paper were put in their stead. This alarm served as a warning of the risks of delaying further[14].

During the following months the Committee set about obtaining estimates for the almshouses. Their method was to draw up a schedule, giving the required dimensions and other particulars of one house and of the 'Great Room' in the centre (which at this date was not intended as a chapel) and then to invite estimates 'in great', that is to say, for the whole of the work necessary for each unit. The advantage of this kind of arrangement was that a single contractor was responsible for the whole job and the Company did not have to co-ordinate the work of a large number of individual craftsmen. It is not clear whether specific contractors were asked to tender for the work, or whether the competition was open. Six contractors delivered their proposals to the Company and these were considered at a committee meeting held on 20 June 1712. The names of the contractors were Mr Burford, carpenter, Mr Sandford, carpenter, Mr Philps, bricklayer, Mr Denning, carpenter, Mr Halsaul, carpenter and Mr Bird, carpenter. Most of them gave separate prices for the Great Room and for one house or 'staircase', but Philps estimated £584 16s 8d for both and Denning's estimate was in the form of a price per square foot. The lowest estimates were submitted by Robert Burford, who proposed to build one staircase for £250 and the Great Room for £320, and Richard Halsaul whose prices were £244 and £347 respectively. After four months had elapsed the estimates were considered by the full Court of the Company and it was resolved that Burford and Halsaul should be 'treated with' about building the almshouses. Finally, on the 10 December 1712 the Committee decided that Burford should build the Great Room and the staircases to the north, while Halsaul should do the staircases to the south. At this stage it was envisaged that there would be five staircases on either side.

By the first week of February 1712/13 the articles of agreement had been prepared and copies were given to the two builders for their consideration. It is evident that the Company must have had access to the services of someone experienced in building, because the agreement was drawn up with scrupulous attention to detail and without any assistance from the contractors. An entry in the committee minutes for the 11 February 1712/13 refers to money 'spent with Colonel Wilkes and Mr Strood settling the scantling, etc, for building the Almshouse', which suggests that these two members of the Committee were very actively involved in the matter; nothing is known of their previous experience, though Strood may be identical with Mr Strode, a bricklayer who was paid for laying the almshouse drains in 1714. The agreement laid down the exact dimensions of the rooms: the Great Room was to be thirty-six feet in frontage, nineteen feet two inches in depth from out to out and seventeen feet eight inches high. The staircases were also to be thirty-six feet in frontage. and eighteen feet in depth, with eight feet six inches clear between floor and ceiling in all rooms. The sizes of the main beams, floor-joists, rafters and even the laths supporting the ceiling were laid down, as well as the size of the nails to be used in securing the laths. Where necessary, the material to be employed was also stipulated; the front walls were to be of good red and grey stock bricks, the main beams, laths, doors, windows and staircases of oak and the floors of yellow deal. The windows of the Great Room were to be filled with best crown glass, the remaining windows with 'castle' glass[15]. The roofs were to be covered with good plain (that is, red) tiles. It was one of the terms of the agreement that examples of the materials intended for use should be produced by the contractors and approved by the Committee.

Some of the exterior features of the building were specifically mentioned. The Great Room was to have a central door with a Portland stone doorcase, with 'rustique' quoins, flanked by round-headed windows. The fenestration of the staircases was indicated on the plan attached to the agreement; each unit was to be five windows wide with a central doorway on the ground floor. All the windows were to be sashes. The Great Room was to have a pitched pediment and there was to be a 'mondelian corniche' across the whole front, made of wood covered with lead. The rear wall was to have a 'covin or plain corniche' much as it has to-day. In front of the building there was to be a paving of Purbeck stone six feet wide.

Many of the interior fittings were also laid down in detail. The Great Room was to be wainscotted, with raised panels ten feet high and a small cornice at the top of the wainscot; the wall above the wainscot was to be plain plastered and whitewashed and the windows were to have inward opening shutters at least seven feet high. The floor was to be of black marble and white Portland or Swedish stone in diagonal squares and, at one end, there was to be a raised mantlepiece 'suitable to the room' and a fire hearth. The fittings of the living rooms were to be similar, though less elaborate; all the rooms and the staircase compartments were to be wainscotted to a height of four feet, with plain plastered and whitened walls above. The windows of the rooms, but not those of the staircase, were to have shutters. In the main living rooms there was to be a plain hearth with a mantlepiece and the small closets opening off each room were each to have a dresser sixteen inches wide and three shelves.

It was agreed that the building work should be completed by the 25 March 1714 and a penalty clause for non-completion was included. The final price settled on was £365 for the Great Room and £248 for each of the staircases, larger sums than either Halsaul or Burford had originally estimated. The number of staircases to be built on each side of the Great Room was increased from five to six. Payment was to be made in five instalments during the course of the work: for the Great Room, one fifth when the brickwork was of sufficient height for the door to be set, two fifths when the ceiling was plastered, the roof tiled and the chimney topped, one fifth when the room had been paved, wainscotted and plastered and the last fifth when the glazing and all other works had been completed. For the staircases, the stages were the completion of the ground floor, the completion of the upper floor, the roofing in, the completion of the internal fittings including the staircases, floor-boards, wainscotting and plastering and the glazing of the windows and the completion of all other works. The last payment was to be made twenty-one days after the completion and the builders could not be held liable for defects thereafter. The agreement was altogether a highly competent document and appears to have been followed to the letter.

The two craftsmen who were party to the agreement are shadowy figures and we do not know very much about them. Richard Halsaul (or Hassall) was a freeman of the Carpenters' Company of London, having been admitted in 1699. He already had some connection with the Ironmongers' Company and, since 1706, had been employed pretty regularly on what was probably routine maintenance work at Ironmongers' Hall. A number of small payments to him are recorded in the accounts for this period but they seldom amount to more than £5 at any one time. Nothing is known of any other work upon which he had been engaged before he agreed to build the almshouses and his premature death in 1714 precluded any subsequent commissions.

Rather more information is available concerning Robert Burford, the other partner in the enterprise. He claimed that Bristol was his town of origin, although there is no record that a Robert Burford was formally apprenticed or admitted to Burgher status in Bristol at any time between 1660 and 1705; nor was he a freeman of the London Carpenters' Company. He was possibly the son of Morrice Burford, carpenter of Bristol, whose son George was bound apprentice to his father in September 1676. The date of Robert Burford's arrival in London is unknown, nor are there any works definitely attributable to him previous to the Geffrye Almshouses. He may have been the same Robert Burford, carpenter, who owned property in the manor of Hampton and was paid for 'looking after several ffountains' at Hampton Court Palace in the 1690s, but no definite connection has been found[16]. The commission from the Ironmongers' Company was probably sufficient to establish him securely in the London building world of the early eighteenth century; there are several indications that he became, in effect, Surveyor to the Company after 1715 and a number of payments to him are recorded for such tasks as inspecting property which the Company was considering for purchase, as well as reporting on the state of buildings and property already in company ownership. Besides his company work, Burford was involved in at least one profitable speculative building enterprise. On 24 May 1716 Dame Margaret Skipwith granted a lease of the three acres of ground called Jockey Field, on the east side of Bedford Row, Holborn, to Burford and George Devall, plumber, 'for improvement of the said premises by building'. Most of the very substantial houses in Bedford Row were undertaken by Burford, while Devall took a greater share in building Great James Street which lay just to the north on another part of Dame Margaret's property[17]. Two of Burford's houses burnt down in 1718, immediately after completion, causing him a loss of £2,837; but he survived this disaster and, by the mid 1720s, had amassed sufficient money to purchase a small country property. In 1723 he bought a three acre field with a cottage in Ballards Lane, near Hampstead Heath, and soon afterwards began to build himself a small country house or villa. The work was interrupted by Burford's untimely death in 1727 when the house was described as 'near completed'. His heirs or executors finished the building, which came to be known as 'Willow Lodge' and survived until 1896, when it was demolished to make way for a housing development.

Burford's will is an interesting document with an element of mystery; the principal legatee was a young woman aged fourteen named Elizabeth Adamson, who had no obvious connections with Burford. She may have been his illegitimate daughter, although there is no indication of this in the will itself. Apart from some small bequests of money and possessions, she was to receive the whole of Burford's estate, amounting to over £6,000. Only in the event of her premature death was the bulk of the money to pass to Burford's sisters, described as 'late of Bristol'. Among the minor legatees were Burford's servant Matthew Chamberlayne, who was to have 'my wearing apparel, books of architecture and two dozen shirts', a number of craftsmen who had presumably been Burford's associates in his building enterprises and the statuary William Palmer. Palmer was also commissioned to make a monument for Burford 'as described by me' to be set up in the church of St George the Martyr, Southwark, but this monument does not appear to have survived[18].

That Burford should commission a monument to his own design from a mason like Palmer, who had a large, if undistinguished, practice, suggests that he considered himself as more than a mere craftsman. That he possessed several books of architecture indicates that he was interested in the theory as well as the practice of building and, if he was indeed working at Hampton Court in the 1690s, he must have known the work of Sir Christopher Wren and his colleagues at first hand. This becomes a matter of some importance when considering the design of the Geffrye Almshouses. In the absence of direct evidence, to whom should the design of the elevations and the layout of the building be attributed?

After reviewing all the information available in the minutes, accounts and other surviving papers, the inescapable conclusion is that the Geffrye's Charity Committee decided on the main elements of the design before any builder was consulted. The idea of a central Great Room, flanked by an equal number of identical staircases, was contained in the initial scheme for which the contractors were invited to tender. Doubtless the Committee was also responsible for determining the general external appearance of the alms-houses by laying down the number of window and door openings and the different architectural ornaments to be used for the Great Room and staircases. The first indication that the former should have a central doorway flanked by round-headed windows, with an overall pediment, was given by the building agreement, which also gave the staircases five-bay fronts. None of the members of the Committee is known to have had particular expertise in architectural matters, but this need not have prevented a committee decision on general questions of planning and design. It was easy enough to follow the example of the many almshouses already built in London. As early as 1704 some members of the Ironmongers' Company had paid a visit of inspection to the Trinity Almshouses in the Mile End Road, presumably in order to gain some idea of the layout and ornament considered suitable for this type of building.

But if the general appearance of the exterior of the new almshouses was dictated by the Committee, there is no doubt that the siting of the buildings and the details of the proportions were decided by Burford. On 24 March 1712/13 the minutes record that 'The Master laid before the Court the scheme drawn by Mr Burford which demonstrated upon which part of the ground he proposes to erect Sir Robert Geffrye's almshouses and in what manner.' Burford also produced a model of the buildings, incorporating some alterations to the Great Room windows from those proposed in the building agreement, and these were accepted by the Court. It is probably safe to assume that the relative size of the various architectural elements such as cornices, windows and doorcases were not decided until this stage.

The design has been called conservative, but the appearance of the almshouses is partly the result of economical budgeting. The main range consists of the Great Room in the centre, with a projecting pedimented front with a small bell turret, flanked by four staircase units, each with a symmetrical five-bay front. A further three staircases of identical appearance enclose the two shorter sides of a large rectangular area, which abuts the east side of the Kingsland Road and is divided from it by a wall and railings. Apart from the Great Room, the buildings have no architectural ornament beyond the conventional timber eaves-cornice. The scale of the buildings is domestic, even though this was one of the largest charitable foundations for the aged in London. The others in what might be described as the First Division: Chelsea Hospital, Greenwich Hospital,

Aske's School and Almshouses in Hoxton and the Trinity Almshouses, could all boast much more in the way of architectural ornament and external pomp. This difference of character was a direct consequence of the terms of Geffrye's will. It will be recalled that the bequest provided for 'as many poor people as the monies arising from the residuary part of my estate may extend or amount unto' and the Committee was clearly uncertain how large a building they could afford. Although the will was not explicit on this point, the Trustees may have considered themselves obliged to provide as much accommodation as possible, at the cost of neglecting appearances.

The difficulties of the trust are well illustrated by the successive increases in the size of the almshouse buildings between 1712 and 1716. The Committee had originally envisaged ten staircases and a Great Room. By the time the building agreement was made the total had been increased to twelve staircases and, shortly after the completion of these buildings, two further staircases were added, making the present number of fourteen. Each additional staircase built added four more pensioners to the foundation and entailed an additional annual expenditure of £27 for their pensions and gowns. The great merit of the design chosen by the Ironmongers was that additions or even demolitions could be made without destroying the symmetrical appearance of the building. In the other charities previously mentioned these problems did not arise; Aske's Almshouses and the Trinity Almshouses catered for a finite number of pensioners (twenty and twenty-eight respectively), while both Greenwich and Chelsea, which did cater for an unspecified number, were financed by the State and did not have to pay such strict attention to cost. It is very much to the credit of the Company that Geffrye's will was interpreted in a way which provided a greater number of places at the expense of architectural display.

The two units of which the design is composed can perfectly well be considered separately. The Great Room has a thoroughly conventional elevation and the ornamental doorway, round-headed windows, angle-quoins, pediment and bell-turret could be paralleled in many other buildings of the late seventeenth and early eighteenth centuries[19]. In fact, the front bears a strong resemblance to the chapel of the Trinity Almshouses, which the Company's officers had been to inspect in 1704, the only major differences being that the Trinity chapel is raised on a semi-basement with an imposing flight of steps before the door, while at the Geffrye almshouses a niche contrived above the doorway to house the statue of the founder, provides an alternative architectural emphasis. The interior of the Great Room was not elaborate. The panelling has already been described and enough survives to make it possible to visualise the appearance of the room before the apse was inserted in the late eighteenth century. Although it was fitted up as a chapel in 1716 the Great Room was originally intended as a court room for the Almshouse Committee, and can never have been entirely satisfactory for its second function.

The 'staircases' are similar to many ordinary houses of the time in their appearance and internal layout although both their description and the provision of equally large rooms on ground and first floor are reminiscent of collegiate buildings. The plan provided a very convenient arrangement for pensioners: four good rooms were provided in each staircase with a small closet opening off the main room and further space in the basement for the storage of fuel and other items. Each room had two large windows opening onto the garden of the almshouses, which gave ample light; one curious feature of the design was that it provided no windows or other openings at the rear of the building, all the closet windows now visible being later insertions. The joinery and fittings were of the current domestic pattern, perhaps slightly old-fashioned in such things as the staircase handrails, and of good quality. Most of them lasted without replacement until the conversion of the buildings in 1911.

Although the executors of Sir Robert Geffrye were determined that the almshouses should make a good display and compelled the Ironmongers to purchase a large and public site, the buildings do not make a strong visual impact. They were arranged, presumably by Robert Burford, round the perimeter of the available land leaving only a narrow strip at the rear of the main range to accommodate privies and a yard. The lowness of the buildings is emphasised by their being set back so far from the road and at present the numerous trees make it difficult to appreciate the appearance of the front, except in winter. On the other hand such an arrangement has great practical advantages: it gives the largest possible amount of open space, which in this case has served at various times as garden, allotments and pasture and, taken together with the windowless rear walls and the high railings towards the road, must have provided a very tolerable enclosed world for the inhabitants of the almshouses.

The building work and the layout of the gardens

Haggerston was a low-lying and marshy area. The ground purchased for the almshouses had a slight slope from east to west and it was necessary for much of the land to be levelled before the building works began. At first the Committee hoped to achieve this by making the site available for refuse tipping; on the 10 July 1712 it was 'ordered that an opening be made in the ground purchased by Sir Robert Geffrye's almshouses for every person that will may shute rubbish thereon at their pleasure.' The tipping continued for over two years but public tipping proved insufficient and it was also found necessary to pay for a large amount of rubbish and soil to be brought in at 2d or 3d each load. On the 18 March 1712/13 the workmen were paid for 'setting out the ground to build at two places', presumably for the separate enterprises of Burford and Halsaul. The slope of the ground made it necessary to build cellars as a first stage because it was essential to place the foundations on firm ground and not on the made up land which had been levelled with rubbish. After the construction of the cellars the work proceeded rapidly. The first payment was made less than two months after commencement, the second a few weeks later and, in August 1713, Mr Halsaul received an extraordinary payment from the Company of £6 to pay for the workmen's raising dinner, which indicates that the southern half of the building had been roofed in. Work continued during the autumn and winter; the interior was fitted by the end of December and the whole building was glazed in and fully finished by April 1714. A shadow was cast over the completion by the death of Richard Halsaul between December 1713 and April 1714, but the final payment was made to his widow on the twenty-third of that month.

While the buildings were going up, many smaller matters were attended to which were outside the main contract. Consideration of a suitable water supply was postponed until the spring of 1714; in April of that year a well-digger named Isaac Eeles offered 'to make two wells at the almshouses, to dig them not less than five feet deep in spring water above ye bottom of ye kerb and six feet wide and to lay the brick, all at £4 7s ye company to be at ye charge of finding brick'; his proposal was accepted. The wells supplied two pumps, which were made by a carpenter named Sears, who was paid for the work in July 1714. In the same month Mr Strode, bricklayer, was paid for making the drains and erecting the two necessary houses or lavatories. Although the almshouses must have been fit for occupation by this time, they remained empty during the autumn of 1714 while the last details were finished; grates for the fireplaces were supplied in November and this is the last such item in the building accounts. On the 15 December the Committee was besieged by 'a great number of persons exhibiting their petitions to be admitted into Sir Robert Geffrye's Almshouses, more than there is room for.' The selection was made with commendable speed and only three days later the sum of 2s 8d was paid 'at setling the almspeople'.

During the following year a series of small building works were carried out, some of which materially affected the functioning of the almshouse and some merely its appearance. Among the latter was the building of the front boundary wall and the provision of railings and gates; on 5 July 1715 'Mr Strodes, Mr Burfords and Mr Sears proposals to inclose Sir Robert Geffrye's Almshouses were read and examined and Mr Burford's best approved of and agreed to with this addition that Mr Burford at his own charge is to provide laths, hinges, locks and bolts necessary and be at the charge of digging and levelling the ground and making ye Company's Armes in ironwork in the middle gates.' Burford's design was 'in faire papire which the committee gave him liberty to take away.' On 9 August, 'the Committee took into consideration ye building of two more staircases at Sir Robert Geffrye's Almshouses and after many reasonings about ye same by vote agreed to proceed in ye building thereof.' One of the extra staircases was to be built by Burford and the other was entrusted to the widow Halsaul, an interesting and unusual example of a female building contractor at this period, albeit on a very small scale. The new additions, which were to be of exactly the same dimensions as the existing staircases, were completed by February 1715/16. Even after close scrutiny of the buildings it is impossible to be sure which are the two extra units. They were probably added to the western end of the two wings; both these staircases (numbers one and fourteen) have a slightly different internal arrangement from the others. In addition to these major works, some small improvements were made to the amenities of the almshouse; the necessary houses were divided and bolts were put on the doors, a stone pavement was laid round the pumps and iron railings were made to lead down from the garden of the almshouses to the back yard.

It must have been in the summer or autumn of 1715 that the Committee finally decided that the Great Room should henceforward serve primarily as a chapel. Robert Burford, acting as the Company's Surveyor, was instructed in August of this year to negotiate for the purchase of a small piece of land on the north side of the almshouse site to serve as a burial ground and, in September, he was ordered to estimate for 'making a reader's desk and seats for a clerk and a pew on both sides and benches round ye Great Room.' The land was purchased for £20 in March 1716[20] and soon afterwards a subscription list was opened 'towards fitting up ye Great Roome at Sir Robert Geffrye's Almshouses for ye use of a chappell'.

The fitting up having been completed, the almshouses remained virtually unaltered for the next two hundred years. The few changes which were made are discussed in the next section of this chapter, but some mention should be made here of the ornaments of the building and of the treatment of the garden.

For the first ten years of the life of the almshouses the only non-architectural ornament was a sun-dial, removed from a house called 'Pogers' in Old Street which belonged to the Ironmongers' Company and was set up, probably inside the pediment, in January 1717/18. The Master in Chancery, directing how Geffrye's bequest should be used, had ordered that 'a handsome effigie of the founder is to be erected in the front or other convenient and proper place'. The statue would have to be paid for out of the income of the charity and it was several years before the primary building costs had been covered. Eventually, in 1723, the question was discussed and on 21 October 'The Court agreed to a modell for ye effigies of Sir Robert Geffrye according to the posture subscribed by the Master' and in the January following, 'Mr Nost agreed to performe the statue of Sir Robert Geffrye six feet high in hard metall in a workmanlike manner and to ffix the same in ye place provided for itt at ye Company's almshouse in Shoreditch, with ye proper ornaments of a Lord Mayor and to give the company a modell thereof in hard metall neatly completed all at forty pounds.' John Van Nost's statue and model have both survived, but neither are at the almshouses; the model is still in the possession of the Ironmongers' Company and the statue now graces the new almshouses at Hook in Hampshire. The present statue on the front of the Museum is a replica made by James Maude and Co, of Mansfield, in 1913. At the same time, the painter Richard Phillips was commissioned to paint a full-length portrait of Robert Geffrye and this very indifferent work also survives in the possession of the Company. It is difficult to believe that these portraits can be a good likeness of the founder of the almshouses, since they were executed twenty years after his death; presumably the portrait at Bethlehem Hospital, painted in Sir Robert's lifetime, was taken as the model for both statues and the painting.

The ornament of the almshouses was completed by the addition of a clock shortly after Van Nost's statue had been set up. In November 1725, the Court debated the question of purchasing a turret clock and it was in position by April 1727. The maker was a Mr Lumpkin; this must have been either Thomas Lumpkin the elder, who was made freeman of the Clockmakers' Company in 1694 and whose name appears on long-case clocks from 1689 onwards, or his son of the same name, who was apprenticed to his father in 1709. The clock seems to have been a poor specimen, for in July 1727 the Clerk of the Company was ordered to acquaint Mr Lumpkin, 'that ye clock at ye Almshouse is continually out of order and that Mr Austen declares he will look after it no longer.'

The land in front of the almshouses is made up ground, levelled by the dumping of rubbish and waste earth. An enormous quantity of such material was brought in between July 1712 and October 1714; more than six-hundred waggon loads were purchased by the Company in addition to what had been tipped when the land was open for public use. When the topsoil was finally brought in, the garden was laid out with lawns and trees. Grass seed for the former was purchased in the spring of 1718/19 and in the autumn of the same year the Committee agreed with a commercial gardener named Longstaffe to plant the staggering number of ninety lime trees on the ground in front of the almshouses. Every tree was to be 'four foot high at the least and in girth or thickness about the bigness of Mr Longstaffe's leg in the small part thereof.' The Company had already paid another gardener called Crapp £1 10s for planting twenty-two lime trees at the back of the almshouse, probably along the ditch which formed the boundary on that side. There is very little hard information available about the layout of the front garden. The earliest known print of the almshouses shows only two squares of lawn on either side of the central pathway; both the trees and front wall are omitted for the sake of clarity. Chassereau's large scale map of the parish of Shoreditch, for which the survey was made in 1745, likewise omits the trees, but shows the main gate set back behind a sweep off the footpath along the side of the Kingsland Road. Probably the best and most reliable guide to the garden layout is the drawing presented to the Company in 1805 by a recently-elected chaplain; besides the gates, walls and railings and the two large lawns the trees are shown in pleached rows along the borders of the lawns. This kind of severely formal arrangement was typical of English gardens in the early eighteenth century and it may well have been the original layout here.

Alterations made to the buildings since 1715

At various times in the last two and a half centuries the buildings of the Geffrye Almshouses have undergone a number of alterations and some rebuilding has been carried out in the present century. It is the object of this chapter to provide a succinct account of the major works, including the removal of parts of the fabric.

Credit must be given to the Ironmongers' Company for the regularity with which the buildings were overhauled while in its ownership. Small items, such as the painting of the woodwork and ironwork, were attended to at frequent intervals, usually every five years. There were also a number of major repairing operations: in the eighteenth century, nearly £250 was expended in 1747 and £208 in 1779 on general repairs and additions and, in 1795, the front gates and railings were renewed at a cost of £119. During the first few years after 1800 it became apparent that the cost of necessary repairs exceeded the income of the charity which could be made available for this purpose and, accordingly, the Company petitioned the Court of Chancery for permission to pay for the work out of its own funds and recoup the money out of the income of the charity over a number of years. Instead, the Master in Chancery proposed a scheme of management which calculated the average outgoings of the charity, reduced the salaries of most of the officers by half and set aside a sum of £50 every year for repairs whether it was required or not. Any surplus was to be paid into a building fund invested in Consols.

A number of calls were made on the building fund in the nineteenth century, several only shortly after it had been established; £252 was spent on repairs in 1816 and £101 in 1817. After this there were no major repairs until 1876 when £3,000 was required for general works. Just before the end of the century the Ironmongers were faced with the necessity of renewing the whole drainage system. The Charity Commissioners were at first reluctant to release the funds for this work and suggested that the Company sell the site in Kingsland Road and move the almshouses to the country, but the Ironmongers were determined to remain in London and eventually obtained sanction for the work in 1896. Having committed themselves to spending nearly £1,000 on the drains, they resolved on a major programme of repairs to put the almshouses in first class condition. Iron tie-rods, bearing handsome Company coats of arms on their plates, were inserted into the walls at various places where they had bulged out of true, much of the internal plasterwork was renewed and in 1898 the roof was repaired and re-covered with new Brosely tiles.

A number of small additions were made while the almshouses were in the care of the Ironmongers. In 1779 the Company Surveyor, who at this date was probably Richard Jupp, was ordered to carry out an unspecified alteration to the committee room at the almshouses, which was almost certainly a reference to the enlargement of one of the downstairs rooms in the staircase south of the chapel. The rear wall was broken through and the room extended into a bow-ended projection which still exists. Over the next few years a number of new furnishings were provided for the new committee room, including a large mahogany table in three sections which could not have been accommodated in a room of ordinary size. In 1797, it was ordered that casement windows should be provided to all the closets which did not already have them. Closet windows were not originally provided for any of the staircases and all of them must be later insertions. At some time in the late eighteenth or early nineteenth centuries, the chapel was improved by the addition of a small apse on the east side with an elegant shell-moulded ceiling. This was probably a consequence of the changing nature of the religious services held in the almshouses. There is good reason to suppose that for most of the eighteenth century there was no provision for Holy Communion, since in 1791 the Company Court specifically ordered 'that an altar for administering the sacraments in the chapel at Sir Robert Geffrye's almshouses be erected agreeable to the plan prepared by the Surveyor.'

Unfortunately, no bill for the work has survived but it is quite possible that, as the Surveyor was involved, the provision of an altar entailed the building of an apse to put it in. Horwood's large scale map of London, published in 1819, does not show the apse but neither does it show the extension of the Committee Room which was certainly in existence by this date. The Company Surveyor in 1791 was Richard Jupp, who had held the post for a number of years although the precise date of his appointment is unknown. Jupp was very much a City architect and most of his commissions came to him through his connections with the great companies. In addition to his appointment with the Ironmongers he was also Surveyor to the East India Company and to Guy's Hospital. His executed work is usually in a restrained classical style, and he was certainly capable of handling the standard architectural vocabulary of the period. The apse of the almshouse chapel, some new chapel fittings and the design of the new gates and railings to the almshouse gardens were the only items of new work he was called upon to execute for the Ironmongers.

In 1881 the benefice of St Dionis Backchurch in the City was united with that of All Hallows Lombard Street and the church of St Dionis itself, where Sir Robert Geffrye and his wife Priscilla were buried, was demolished. One consequence was that the charity income set aside for the saying of daily prayers reverted, under the terms of Geffrye's will, to Bridewell and Bethlehem Hospitals. The Ironmongers contested the case in Chancery in an attempt to retain control of the money but without success. The bodies of Sir Robert and his wife were removed from the chancel of the church and re-interred in the almshouse burial ground, where their grave is now marked by a graceless stone tomb. The fine marble monument in the church was dismantled and re-erected in the almshouse chapel. It was again removed in 1911 and set up in the chapel of the Company's new almshouses at Mottingham, but has now been restored to the Museum.

Tucked inconspicuously at the east end of the south range is the Victoria Room, the only major addition to the almshouses, which was designed by Mr Richard Roberts, Company Surveyor, in 1896 and completed in the spring of 1897. Although it was named in the year of the Queen's Diamond Jubilee, the room was not built specifically as a memorial. Towards the end of 1895, a suggestion was made to the Company Court that No. 1 staircase, which had until recently been occupied by the almshouse chaplain and his family, should be converted to serve as a recreation room for the pensioners. The idea was rejected as too expensive, as was a subsequent suggestion that the Matron's lodgings be used for the purpose and the Surveyor was instructed to investigate other ways of providing suitable accommodation. He suggested that an entirely new room be provided for the purpose and, somewhat inconsistently, the

Court agreed. The final design was approved in the spring of 1896; building began in September and the Committee of Trust Supervisors held their first meeting in the new room on 25 March 1897. The work cost £395. As we have seen, 1896 had been an expensive year for the charity, which had been obliged to pay nearly £1,000 for a new drainage system and it was doubtless for this reason that the idea of naming the room after the Queen was seized on as an economical means of marking the Jubilee year. Mr Roberts' new building was designed in an early eighteenth century style with heavy bracketted doorcase and a hipped roof; now that the red brick has weathered it blends well with the older buildings.

As a result of the extensive repairs carried out by the Company in the preceding twenty years, the almshouses were in excellent condition when they were acquired by the London County Council in December 1911. It was originally intended to continue to use the buildings as houses, but as soon as the decision was taken to use them for a public museum it was inevitable that some alterations would have to be made. Fortunately, the Architect's Department, headed by W. E. Riley, favoured a conservative approach and a report made in connection with a scheme for conversion which was presented in December 1911, emphasised that 'it is important that in any scheme to adapt these buildings for the purposes indicated there should be the least possible interference with the old work, either as to taking from it or adding to it. This prohibition applies more especially to the chapel.' But the same report conceded that the stairs were very narrow, with a large number of winders, and could only be used by persons in single file. The proposed scheme involved the removal of the partition walls of the upper storey and of most of the stairs between ground and first floor, producing two floors of exhibition space. In the event, a more drastic course was followed and the stairs, staircases, partition-walls and upper floors of the central block were all removed. The brick party walls between the houses were retained, but were cut through at ground level to provide direct access from one room to the next. The main joists of the upper floor were allowed to remain to give some stiffening, but even these were eventually replaced by iron ties. In accordance with the architect's recommendations, the chapel was left intact; the party walls were not cut through and, instead, an open timber gallery was built round the apse to allow visitors to pass from one side of the main range to the other. The proposals were approved in March 1912 and had been completed by October 1913.

The two wings were not altered at first, but a second series of alterations in 1925 transformed the north wing into additional exhibition space and part of the south wing into a lecture hall. At the same time covered passages were built to link the main range with the wings. Shortly after the Second World War several parts of the structure were found to be in poor condition. The slight bulging of the external walls, particularly in the north wing, which had been remarked at the end of the nineteenth century, appeared to have worsened sufficiently to cause alarm. The removal of the stiffening provided by the floors and stairs was probably the main reason for the deterioration, but the foundations had also been shaken by the blast from bombs dropped in the vicinity of the almshouses. The job of rectifying the defects was not undertaken by the Council, but entrusted to the firm of H. S. Goodhart-Rendel and Partners, one of the more distinguished architectural practices of the time, with considerable experience of the problems of old buildings. Under their supervision the entire front wall of the north wing and of the northern half of the main range was rebuilt, new lavatory blocks were provided in the angles between the main range and the wings, the walls of the chapel were finally cut through to give direct access from one end of the main range to the other and the timber gallery behind the chapel was glazed-in. Since these alterations there have been only minor works: the lecture hall in the south wing was re-converted as a gallery for small exhibitions in 1975 and the front railings were renewed at the same time.

Of the original almshouse accommodation, only the chapel and No 14 staircase, which serves as the Head Attendant's house, have survived more or less intact. One of the upper rooms in No 13 staircase also contains some original fittings and from these it is still possible to obtain a reasonably accurate picture of the original appearance of the rooms. Perhaps a last word should be said here about the garden of the almshouses which has suffered as much change as the building. At the beginning of the nineteenth century the layout was still formal, though it appears that the lawns were sometimes used for grazing sheep or growing potatoes. By the 1860s the large lawn had been subdivided by lateral paths branching off the main approach and flanked by herbaceous beds for most of their length; the trees were still ranged around the edge of the lawn but it must have been at about this time that plane trees were introduced instead of the original lime trees. Only three limes still remain. After the LCC takeover, the old beds were swept away, the central part of the garden was paved and a small pond created just in front of the chapel. A bust of Sir William Cremer, the local Member of Parliament who had campaigned for the retention of the almshouse garden, was set up on the west side of the pond. Several of the trees appear to have been cut down at about this time. A description of the garden written in 1921 is fulsome in its praise of the facilities; 'Geffrye in his acre-and-a-quarter has given them not only a museum but also a playground. On goodly wooden benches they may sit and breathe and see the sky. Here also is a bandstand, and once a week Shoreditch dances. Not on the grass, for that tender herb needs all the strength Nature can give, simply to live; but on a paved part widened for the purpose. Over the door is a be-wigged statue of Geffrye. Dancers, as you foot it, turn your eyes to him once, and say "Thank you, Sir Robert!"' The bandstand was doubtless removed in the Second World War, which also brought an air-raid shelter which still lies beneath the turf on the south side of the garden, but post-war policy has brought the garden back almost to the charming appearance which it had just before the almspeople left.

Chapter three

The inhabitants
of the almshouses

The inhabitants

Sir Robert's bequest had been unusually generous in intention. His hospital was to be for the benefit of poor people without distinction and he imposed no restrictive conditions of entry. Although it was clearly an almshouse in the accepted sense, one cannot help wondering whether Geffrye himself had not envisaged an institution which would be similar to the great hospitals established in the sixteenth century for the sick and insane. If these were his intentions his will was not sufficiently explicit to put them into effect. His bequests were interpreted by his trustees in a thoroughly conventional way. The second clause of the rules for governing the almshouses, which were promulgated in 1715, declared:

'That any relation of the said benefactor that is a proper object, shall be preferred to any other petitioner: and in defect of any such relation petitioning, it is ordered that any member or their widow that have been Liverymen or Freemen of the Company of Ironmongers', who is a proper object, shall be preferred to any other petitioner: but in defect of any such petitioning, the greatest object that shall petition shall be chosen without favour or affection.' As a result, the occupants were divided from the beginning into two classes, those who were free of the Company and those who had no connection with it, although both classes received the same pension of £6 a year.

No doubt the Company would have preferred to have only freemen and their widows in the hospital, but there was so large a number of places available that it is unlikely that there was ever a sufficient number of suitable candidates to make this possible. Nevertheless, the minutes of the Almshouse Committee constantly re-asserted that free persons were to be given preference over all other petitioners for relief. In 1811, a Chancery Master charged to enquire into the running of the almshouses suggested that more non-free persons be considered for entry but his advice had no effect. Only once, in 1823, was this exclusiveness endangered by a recommendation from the Company Court to the Almshouse Committee that places should be bestowed 'on the most necessitous candidate from age or infirmities', but the following year it was invalidated by a resolution that, 'those persons in the almshouse not free of the Company do resign their rooms when free persons apply for admission.'

There is no information about the proportions of free and non-free inhabitants at the almshouses in the first hundred years; they are all described in the accounts simply as 'pensioners'. In 1834, however, there were twenty-three non-free persons resident and thirty-two free persons and their wives. By 1892 the number of free persons had decreased to only seventeen and there were still the same number of non-free. The alteration in the proportions of free and non-free inhabitants happened only gradually during the course of the nineteenth century but by the end of this period the non-free were always in the majority. Many of the London almshouse charities were faced with a similar shortage of company members and for several of them this was a serious problem. In some instances, where the entrance qualifications were very restrictive, no suitably qualified recipients could be found and in default of pensioners the trustees were forced to rent out the almshouse accommodation to any who would have it. A striking example of this difficulty is afforded by the Framework Knitters' almshouses, which stood immediately to the north of the Geffrye almshouses. The terms of the original trust had laid down that the twelve occupants of the building should be chosen from members of the company resident within five miles of London. By 1900 the industry had removed to Nottingham and Leicester, leaving hardly a single stocking-loom in London, and it often happened that none of the occupants of the almshouses was a member of the Company. Eventually the Framework Knitters obtained permission to break the trust under *cy-pres*, sold the London site and used part of the proceeds to build new almshouses at Oadby in Leicestershire. Transfers for similar reasons became common after 1850, but fortunately the flexibility of Geffrye's bequest made such strangulation impossible.

In theory, the almshouses could hold fifty-six people, allowing one person to each room, although the possible maximum was affected by the practice, at certain periods, of setting aside more than one room for the use of the resident officers and allowing the spouses or children of pensioners to share their room. When the almshouses opened in December 1714, forty-three people were admitted. For the next thirty years the numbers fluctuated between thirty-nine and fifty-one; the variation can be attributed to deaths, one or two expulsions and the occasional oversight in not filling places. There had been a great number of applicants for the first places and it is clear that there was no falling off in the demand. In 1728 the Court received thirty-seven applications for only eight places. After 1740, however, the number of pensioners admitted began to decline rapidly; in 1749 there were only fourteen people on the Foundation, and in 1754 only eight.

The most likely reason for this alteration in the establishment is the unhappy state of the finances of the Charity. Either as a consequence of the repair work undertaken in the mid 1740s or for some other reason, the Committee found itself unable to meet all the expenses of the almshouses out of the income produced by the Charity's property. Insufficient endowment was a common stumbling block for almshouse trustees, especially in those cases where the original donor had made no specific provision for maintaining the buildings.

Geffrye's will had directed that repairs should be paid for out of the regular annual income, but the rental from stock and from the houses in the Strand, which at this date were the principal endowment of the Charity, did not show a high enough return to cover extraordinary costs. In this instance the Committee were forced to borrow from Company funds and continued to do so at intervals throughout the eighteenth century. The problem was only solved by the increase in London property values and rents during the following century. After 1755, the number of pensioners began to rise again and in 1766 the Committee passed a resolution that, in view of the improved financial state of the Charity, the regular complement should be raised from nineteen to twenty-five, which remained the usual number for the next seventy years. A scheme of management, approved by Chancery Decree in 1811, confirmed that twenty-six pensioners was the maximum number which the finances of the charity could support. A second scheme was prepared in 1835 which, on the basis of the improved finances, recommended that the number of pensioners on the foundation be increased from twenty-six to forty-two; thenceforward there were usually about forty pensioners in residence.

In later years the number of occupants was virtually identical with the number of pensioners, but this had not always been the case. Married couples, of whom only the husband was a pensioner, were occasionally admitted and there are numerous examples of residents who lived with their children; some of these were young children, not of an age to work, but others were fully-grown. There is also good reason to suppose that non-pensioners sometimes occupied rooms at the almshouse, despite the ruling of the Court in August 1722 'that noe person shall be admitted to dwell in Sir Robert Geffrye's Almshouses but who shall be choosed by a Court as an almsman or almswoman'. As the finances of the Charity worsened the Committee was perhaps more willing to allow non-pensioners to occupy the building. In 1746 it was ordered 'that all persons who now inabit any of the Company's almshouses in Kingsland Road without any order of this Court for that purpose be forthwith dismissed.' Similar admonitions re-occur at intervals in the second half of the century, but even as late as 1820 there were nine women at the almshouse who are described as 'inmates' and who were neither free of the Company nor on the Foundation. At the same date there were seven married couples resident, excluding the chaplain's family.

Female occupants were always in the majority. Thirty-five women and eight men were admitted in 1715; a century later there were seven men and nineteen women and in 1892 only three men and thirty-eight women. There was nothing unusual about such an imbalance. Geffrye's will had not made any stipulation about the sex of the recipients of his charity and even in those other foundations where it was intended that there should be equal numbers of men and women, parity was seldom maintained. This was true not only of Shoreditch, but of all London, if not all England. In Shoreditch there were, at various times, five almshouses exclusively for women but only two for men (one of which was always occupied by women) and most of the mixed foundations were monopolised by the female sex. Why should there have been an imbalance of this kind? No doubt the principal reason was that there was always a vastly greater number of female applicants for places. Women usually live longer than men and, as a result, there must always have been a larger number of elderly women in need of relief. In the nineteenth century roughly half of the occupants of the Geffrye almshouse were women who had outlived their husbands. Old men could often support themselves with their earnings but the work available to elderly widows and spinsters did not usually pay very well; there was little choice beyond housework and needlework and the latter was notoriously underpaid. Without the support of a family it might be impossible to earn enough to pay for even the bare necessities of life. Perhaps, too, a measure of sentiment was allowed to influence the choice of the Committee; this was almost certainly true in the nineteenth century when an increasing number of the applicants for charity were women of genteel upbringing and of the same social class as the members of the Committee themselves.

When we come to consider the character of the people admitted to the almshouses we are on treacherous ground. The main source of information is in the records of the Committee and those of the Company Court, both of which are apt to record misbehaviour and deviations from normal conduct, rather than adherence to it. The day book, in which a record of minor transgressions was kept, has not survived. It is probably true to say that the eighteenth century occupants were more unruly than their nineteenth-century successors; more offences were recorded in the first hundred years of the alms-houses than in the second. At a court held on 16 October 1721, 'Joseph Stanley one of the Almsmen, appeared and was charged with being drunk and helping Ffield another almsman also drunk over ye almshouse wall at an unreasonable time of night and then neglecting him and suffering him to lye soe long on the ground yt he soon after dyed.' In 1727 two women were brought before the Court for scolding together; a widow was expelled from the almshouse in 1723 for harbouring her daughter, 'a person of bad character' and in 1787 Thomas Tillinghurst was expelled for wife-beating. Only the last of these could be described as a serious crime and the number of misdemeanours recorded over two hundred years is surprisingly small.

There can also be little doubt that the eighteenth-century occupants were generally not very well-off. The annual stipend of £6 had been a fairly lowly allowance in 1704 and although some of the pensioners received a supplement from Thomas Betton's charity, which was established in 1723, many of them had to exist on their basic allowance. The £6 had only to pay for food and some clothes, since all other necessities were supplied by the charity but, as the cost of food steadily increased during the eighteenth century, the pension must have seemed less and less adequate. In 1810 the pension was increased, or at least it was ordered that any surplus income from the estate, remaining after essential expenses had been paid, should be distributed as pensions, up to a maximum of £16. The average annual pension after this date seems to have been about £8. As the nineteenth century progressed the basic pension was improved by a series of small bequests until, by the end of the century, free inmates received an average of £27 19s 3d per year, and the non-free inmates £29 2s 2d; still not large sums, but adequate for essentials[21].

From the 1840s it was made a condition of entry to the almshouses, for people who were not free of the Ironmongers' Company or widows of freemen, that they should have an income of at least 5s a week, either from their own resources or guaranteed by friends. This regulation had a significant effect on the social composition of the Foundation, bringing in an increasing number of occupants who could be loosely described as genteel. One instance may suffice to illustrate this change. At the time of the census of 1861 four of the occupants described their former occupation as schoolmistress or governess; by 1892 there were ten occupants under this heading. During the public enquiry concerning the future of the almshouse, held in 1908, the matron observed of the inmates that, 'The great majority are persons who have been accustomed to refinement either in homes of their own or in some other capacity in the houses of others'. But it would be wrong to assume that decayed gentlefolk had completely ousted the working class element. At the close of the century there were still a number of occupants who had been employed in menial work; in 1892 there were four who had been in service, four who had been employed in some branch of the dress-making industry and six who were described as 'widows without means'. Nevertheless, there is no doubt that the social class of the occupants was gradually improving during the second half of the nineteenth century.

The amenities of the building

The Charity was required to provide accommodation, a pension and 15s for a gown for each inhabitant of the almshouses; these requirements remained constant for the whole life of the Foundation in London. The accommodation provided for each pensioner consisted of one room, thirteen feet in front, fifteen feet broad and eight feet six inches high, with two large sash windows overlooking the garden. On one of the longer sides, opposite the door, was a fireplace with a mantlepiece over it. Opening off the rear of the main room was a smaller room or closet, four feet six inches by three feet six, tucked behind the staircase. To begin with, the closets were windowless, but some windows were cut through the back walls during the eighteenth century and in 1797 it was ordered that windows were to be provided for all closets. On one side of the closet was a dresser, and there were also three shelves; none of these dressers has survived[22]. The main room had to serve for all purposes of living, including sleeping, cooking and washing. No other living facilities were provided before 1897, when the Victoria Room was built as a day room and social focus.

No furniture of any kind was provided by the charity except what was fixed to the walls. It is difficult to believe that some basic items, a bed and a chair for example, were not provided for the very poorest pensioners, but there is nothing in the Company records to suggest that such was the case. Indeed, it looks as though the Company regarded the possessions of the occupants as a security for good conduct and also for the cost of their burial. Rule XIV states that 'the burial charges for any pensioners dwelling within the almshouses shall be defrayed by their friends and relatives before they move their goods', implying that in default of payment the goods might be sold for the purpose. Probably a small stock of furniture was built up from items not claimed by friends and relations which could supply what was needed by very poor arrivals.

As an exception to their general rule, the Committee did agree to provide furnishings for the resident chaplain and a list of the objects provided has fortunately survived. The list was compiled in 1732, when the chaplain occupied only two rooms. Besides the bedstead with its linen and blankets, the rooms contained '4 cane chairs, 2 cane elbow chairs, 1 wallnutt tree table and an iron stove grate and fender'.[23] The rooms of the pensioners presumably contained even less than this; a bed, table, chair and some utensils for cooking and eating would be sufficient and not much different from the usual furniture of a poor person's dwelling of the time. In the next century matters must have improved, as furniture became cheaper and some of the occupants relatively wealthier than they had been before. No illustration of the interiors of these rooms has survived, but, by the mid-nineteenth century, they were probably not unlike the usual cluttered cottage living room, with the addition of a bed. By 1900 all the rooms had gas-light and a sink (without a tap) had been installed in the closet, but otherwise there were few improvements.

Besides the living room and closet, each occupant had a part of the basement in which to keep the annual allowance of coal supplied by the Company. From the beginning, the coal stores had lockable doors to prevent pilfering. The cellar also contained a copper for boiling water. All other cooking had to be done on the hob in the living room. This sounds a cumbersome arrangement, but hob grates were in common use long after the introduction of the cooking range and, in 1900, there were still a very large number of households in England without any apparatus designed specifically for cooking food. When the architect W. D. Caroe inspected the almshouses for the Charity Commissioners in 1909 he commented 'I think that more convenient cooking and heating stoves might with advantage be put in, although the type of hob grate now in use is good and sound in itself.'[24] The form of the original grates provided at the almshouses is uncertain. The surviving grates used by the pensioners, one of which is now in the Director's room, appear to date from the 1840s.

No meals of any kind were paid for by the charity, except on special occasions, such as the Jubilee of Queen Victoria, and all food had to be provided by the occupants. Invalid occupants sometimes had also to pay for their food to be cooked and water brought up, either by another pensioner or by someone from outside the almshouses.

None of the rooms had running water. At first, water was obtained from two wells in the back yard behind the main range; it had to be pumped up from the wells by hand and transported to the living-room in a pail. In 1739 the Company made enquiries about the possibility of obtaining a supply of water from the New River Company, whose reservoirs were a short distance away at Sadler's Wells. Next year it was ordered that a supply should be laid on at an annual cost of £6. The supply was brought to a pump in the yard, possibly one of the pumps which had previously served a well, and the pensioners still had to ferry all their water for drinking, cooking and washing in a bucket up to their rooms, and then carry the slops down to the drain in the basement. Even so, New River water was something of a luxury and usually reserved for the better-off private customers who could afford it. The almspeople were not slow to cash-in on their new supply and, only two months after installation, the Ironmongers' Company was forced to pass an order that the water should not be re-sold to strangers. Theft of water was also a real possibility and the pump was kept locked as a precaution. Each occupant had their own key, which was produced and shown to the Committee on the four quarter-days when the pension instalments were paid over. In the 1870s, a supply of mains water was brought to the almshouse and a single cold water tap installed in the basement of every staircase; this arrangement continued until the closure of the almshouses.

At about the same time that the water supply was brought into the buildings, the lavatories were improved. Originally there had been only two of them, intended to serve the whole almshouse, situated at the north end of the back yard. Cleaning the lavatories, or 'necessary houses' as they were called, was one of the tasks of the ground keeper and in the early years he probably emptied their contents into the ditch along the rear boundary. By 1868 each staircase had been provided with its own lavatory in a small back extension, reached by way of the basement. The cleansing arrangements were still quite primitive, however, and one inmate recalled that even after 1900 the drains were flushed once a week from a cistern situated in the roof of the chapel.

Besides the lavatories and pumps the back yards also contained the laystalls or rubbish bins. All the occupants were required to place their rubbish in these receptacles which were emptied periodically by the Ground Keeper. Such a concentration of essential services was functional but presented health-risks. It was nevertheless not uncommon for lavatories and drinking water supply to be placed near each other. Not until the researches following the dreadful cholera epidemics of the 1830s and 1840s was the nature of the risk of pollution generally realised.

Very little is known about the gowns which were provided by the Company in accordance with the founder's will. No examples have survived, nor are there any illustrations which show one in use. All that can be said with certainty is that the gowns were blue in colour. Paupers commonly had clothing of blue or brown stuff because the sources of these dyes were easily come by and therefore cheap. The source of blue dye was woad, the same plant

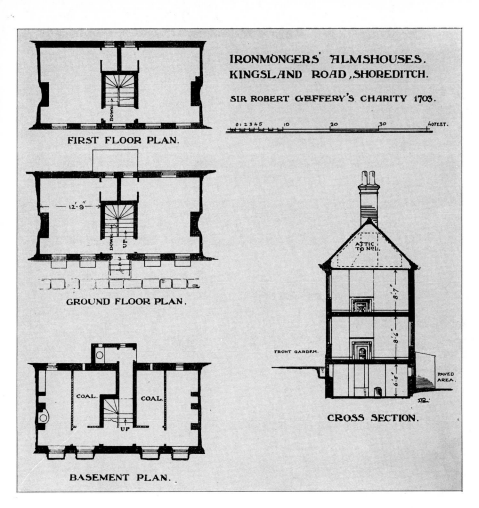

IRONMONGERS' ALMSHOUSES.
KINGSLAND ROAD, SHOREDITCH.

SIR ROBERT GEFFERY'S CHARITY 1703.

FIRST FLOOR PLAN.

GROUND FLOOR PLAN.

BASEMENT PLAN.

CROSS SECTION.

(Below) An early engraved view of the buildings, from William Maitland's History of London from its foundation by the Romans to the present time. Second edition 1756.

(Above) Plans and a section of one of the staircases, drawn for Volume VIII of the Survey of London

WE, the Churchwardens and Overseers of the Poor of the Parish of *St Saviour Southwark* and other Parishoners of the said Parish, whose Names are hereunto subscribed, do severally promise and agree to and with the Master and Keepers or Wardens and Commonalty of the Mystery or Art of IRONMONGERS, of the City of *London*, That if they will be pleased to elect and place *Mary Courtney widow* ——————————— Inhabitant in the Parish aforesaid, as an Alms *woman* —— into *Sir Robert Geffery's* Alms-Houses, in *Kingsland Road*, in the Parish of *St. Leonard, Shoreditch*, in the County of MIDDLESEX; and if after such Admission, the said *Mary Courtney* ——————————— shall happen to die, and not be removed from the said Alms-House, that We, the said Churchwardens, Overseers, and Parishoners, or our Successors shall and will pay the Charges and Expences of the Burial of the said *Mary Courtney* ——————

And if after such Admission the said *Mary Courtney* ——————————— shall be expelled and removed therefrom, that We, the said Churchwardens, Overseers, and Parishoners, or our Successors, shall and will receive and take the said *Mary Courtney* ——————————— into the said Parish, and there to be provided for as *a* poor Inhabitant of the said Parish. Witness our Hands, this *twenty fifth* Day of *July* —— **1800**

Tho Amphlet } CHURCHWARDENS.

R Dawson
Wm Knott } OVERSEERS.
Jonath Harris

Edwd T Bishop & Banks } PARISHONERS.
Edwd Sills

A petition for admission to the almshouses.

The portrait of Sir Robert Geffrye, reputedly painted by Sir Godfrey Kneller for Bridewell Hospital: now at King Edward's School, Witley.

Peter Chassereau's
map of the parish
of Shoreditch, made
in 1745: the Geffrye
Almshouses appear
as No. 6 in the key.

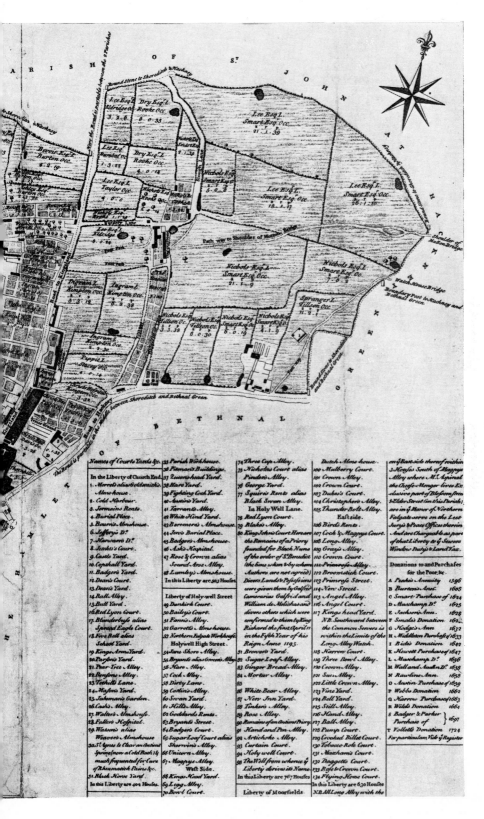

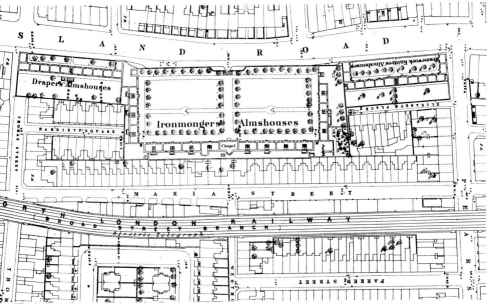

(Top of facing page) The interior of the chapel in 1906.

(Bottom of facing page) The Director's Room: showing the original wainscotting and one of the fireplaces used by the almspeople.

(Top of this page) The timber gallery round the chapel, constructed by the LCC in 1914.

(Bottom of this page) The almshouses and their immediate surroundings, from the Ordnance Survey of 1870.

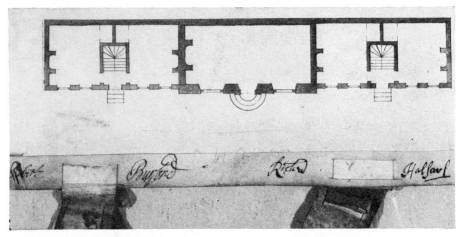

(Top) Ground plan of the Great Room and two staircases attached to the original building agreement, with the signatures of Robert Burford and Richard Halsaul.

(Bottom) The site of the almshouses advertised for sale in The Times, *11 August 1906* page 14.

the subjects of Boadicea had used to stain their bodies when preparing for battle with Julius Caesar. The best known examples of blue pauper clothing are probably the 'bluecoat school' charities, which spread all over the country in the wake of Edward VI's Christ's Hospital, but almspeople often had garments of this colour. Both the pensioners and the scholars of Aske's Hospital in Hoxton, for example, had gowns of light blue. At the Ironmongers' almshouses the traditional colour persisted even after the provision of clothing had been commuted to a money payment. As late as 1906 an observer remarked, 'There were many quaint rules and regulations originally; some have been done away with, but some still remain in force, one being that the women must have at least one blue dress, to be worn at stated times.'[25]

What would their gowns have looked like? Charity costume was always conservative and also plain, designed to give no possible cause for vanity. After about 1600, a 'gown' for men usually meant something like the academic gowns still worn today at University functions which is based on the standard outer garment of Tudor times, open at the front and falling to mid-calf, with large and pendulous sleeves. It must have had only limited usefulness and was probably soon relegated to be worn on special occasions only. Gowns for women were more useful; made like dresses, they provided a sufficient and substantial outer garment and generally copied the shape of the examples current fifty years previously. In most cases, the outer clothing of charity women consisted of a gown, a shawl and a bonnet. There is no reason to doubt that the inmates of the Geffrye almshouses followed this pattern and photographs of the old ladies taken in the first decade of this century show them wearing all three.

It is doubtful whether Geffrye's bequest was for long sufficient to pay the full cost of the gowns, at least for the women. Even the standard unadorned women's gowns of the early eighteenth century required eight to ten yards of material and, in addition, the cost of making up had to be found. Garments were certainly provided by the Company in the first half of the eighteenth century, because the bills survive, but by 1860 the provision of gowns had been commuted to a money payment of 15s. All other clothing had to be found by the pensioners themselves. With a new gown each year it must often have been possible to re-use the old material and, indeed, in January 1715 the almspeople were directed by the Committee to make petticoats out of their old gowns.

The only other material comfort provided was the pension. Sir Robert had ordered that £6 a year be given to each pensioner in four instalments on the four quarter-days. The subsequent increases made to this sum have already been mentioned. No rules were imposed as to whether or not an inmate might receive an income additional to the pension nor was any explicit restriction made on the wealth of an inhabitant when once admitted. Some of the eighteenth-century residents almost certainly had their own means and some in the nineteenth century had small private incomes, but it may be presumed that many of those who received the pension were wholly dependent on it and received nothing else, apart from the small amount they might earn by casual work. With their pension the almspeople had to purchase all their food for the year, candles for lighting and any clothing necessary besides the gowns. These were the basic necessities of life, but money might also be required to purchase or replace some furnishings or to pay for small luxuries such as tobacco or needles. Like most similar benefactors, Geffrye had doubtless intended to provide for a very frugal lifestyle, with no opportunity for rash spending. It is difficult to say what sort of existence one could have had on £6 a year in 1714, when the first almspeople were admitted. W K Jordan, in his massive study of philanthropy in England, remarks that over the whole of the period between 1480 and 1660 the average annual stipend for occupants of almshouses in the London area was £4 4s a year. Although bene-factions had risen slowly over the period, there was no regularity about the process. For example, the occupants of Thomas Sutton's large foundation of the Charterhouse, which was established in 1611, were allowed £5 per annum; nearly one hundred years earlier Henry VIII had allowed the seven decayed men who occupied the Woostaple Almshouses £5 6s. Samuel Harwar, who established twelve almshouses on the south side of Geffrye's in 1703, left his pensioners 2d a day with an additional shilling and load of coal yearly. The £6 a year allowed by Sir Robert in his will in 1704 may not have been notably generous, but it was probably an adequate living allowance, at least in the early years of the almshouses.

Some aspects of life in the almshouses

The pace of life in an institution occupied mainly by the elderly was doubtless slow and a pensioner's existence uneventful. The constraints on the pensioners at the Geffrye almshouses were not severe. There were no set times for meals and few compulsory activities. Certain duties and limitations of freedom were, however, imposed by the Company rules. In November 1714 the Committee paid 13s 6d 'for a coppye of ye Salters' orders about yr. Almshouses at Maidenhead' as a basis for discussion and, one year later, the Ironmongers' own rules were approved by the Company Court. There were originally twenty-nine ordinances, the full text of which is given in Appendix I. They seem to have excited much admiration; Seymour declared that they should be 'set down for good Example sake and for the good of any other well-disposed persons, that are, or shall be minded to lay out their Christian Charity that way.'[26] The original rules may seem harsh, but they were intended to guard against the abuses which were common enough in some other almshouse foundations. Only a few people were ever expelled. During the course of the nineteenth century the rules were revised on at least two occasions, each time in the direction of greater leniency.[27]

Rule VII affirmed that the service of God was to be above all things respected. Attendance at church on Sunday was always compulsory and the pensioners were also to attend public worship on days of public thanksgiving. Although it was ordered that they should go 'either to their parish church, or to some other place where Divine service to Almighty God is performed', it must have been customary, from the beginning, for pensioners to attend the ordinary services in the almshouse chapel and not those held in the parish church. Only a Sunday service was held in the early eighteenth century, but by the 1790s the number of compulsory services had been increased; besides the Sunday service there were also Morning Prayers on Wednesday and Friday. The Sunday services were in the afternoon, except for the first Sunday in each month, when the service of Communion began at 11.00 a.m.

One striking feature of the original rules is the emphasis on the need for clean living. Bearing in mind that the almspeople were all supposed to be over fifty-six years of age, it is surprising to find no less than four rules concerned with adultery, lewdness and the avoidance of 'unquiet persons'. Tidiness was also requisite and rule XVII ordered that the almspeople should 'keep their rooms and the walks ways and passages before their doors sweet and clean'. In 1752, this direction was made more specific and it was given out that the almspeople must 'every Saturday sweep their doors and take away the dirt, and that they do not throw bones and raggs on the grass plots.'

Absence overnight was not permitted, unless with the approval of the Company officers. Permission for prolonged leave of absence was never given in the eighteenth century and a number of almshouse residents were expelled for being away too long. This rule was relaxed in the nineteenth century and, by 1886, each pensioner was allowed a maximum of four weeks leave at the discretion of the matron. Pensioners were also required to be in the almshouses by a certain time every evening. The first rules ordered 'that all persons belonging to the said almshouses, shall return, and come to their severall lodgings ... between the first day of October, to the first day of March yearly at or before the hour of seven o'clock in the evening, of these days; and between the first day of March and the first day of October, yearly, at, or before the hour of nine o'clock'. By the 1880s, pensioners were only required to be within the gate of the almshouses by ten o'clock, winter and summer. At the appointed time the front gate of the almshouses was shut and locked. The only keys were held by the chaplain, the matron and the ground keeper.

Four times a year, as nearly as possible on the four Quarter days, the Almshouse Committee paid a formal visit. These visits had the twofold purpose of distributing the benefits of the Charity and considering any breach of the rules. On every quarter day £1 10s in gold was given to each of the pensioners and, on Lady Day, new gowns were issued, or the money paid in the stead of gowns. Both of these ceremonies took place in the committee room on staircase No 8, on the south side of the chapel, although for the last few years in Shoreditch, when public transport between Haggerston and the City was rapid and frequent, pensions were paid at the Hall. At the spring and autumn visitations, the rules were read out in full to the almspeople during the course of a service in the chapel. Any minor offences committed during the preceding three months were punished on the spot. In most cases the punishment was in the form of a fine which could be deducted out of the pension. One third of the fine was paid to the informant and two thirds into the poor box in the chapel. More serious offences, including any which carried the penalty of expulsion, had to be referred to one of the General Company courts. Expulsion, when it was imposed, took effect at once; the culprit was locked out of his or her room and their goods transferred to the cellar under the chapel to await collection. Anyone who had been expelled could not be re-admitted.

Within these limits the almspeople were left to themselves. Doubtless many of them, especially the older ones, were content to gossip and enjoy the garden. Others took small jobs to supplement their pension. The rules forbade the practice of any trade or occupation which might annoy the other occupants, or which would involve the assistance of another person, but it is plain that the Trustees were content to allow the pensioners to work and even encouraged them. Before the site in Haggerston had been chosen, one of the arguments put forward by the Trustees in favour of a site nearer the City was 'that the poor people may with great ease and convenience provide themselves of all necessities for their living and may have frequent opportunities to employ themselves and be industrious in usefull and beneficiall occupations for the good of themselves and the public'. Several jobs were available within the almshouse itself and these are dealt with separately in the next section of this chapter. The most usual ways of making money for women were by such occupations as sewing and child-minding, both of which could be carried on without assistance. We have already seen that a number of the nineteenth-century occupants had been seamstresses of some kind before their admission and sewing, paid at piecework rates, lent itself very well to the life of the almspeople. Child-minding might be thought less suitable, but it was certainly undertaken by some pensioners for, in 1781, a Mrs Morris was directed by the Committee 'not to continue the nurse-child she has had for some time past.' It is probable that the taking of outside employment was more characteristic of the eighteenth century than the nineteenth, since retired schoolmistresses and ladies with secured incomes were less likely to need the income from casual work, but it may never have died out completely.

Several entries in the Court minutes prove that livestock was kept and food-stuffs grown, at various times, on the ground belonging to the almshouses. Poultry was kept throughout the eighteenth century in the back yard and, at the beginning of the nineteenth century, both cows and sheep were allowed to be grazed on the lawns. It is possible that the larger animals were only kept as a means of obtaining cheaper food during the period of chronic inflation caused by the Napoleonic wars and the same motive probably led the Court to order, in 1816, that some of the ground in front of the almshouses should be planted with potatoes. Certainly the land had not always been used for grazing, since it was named as one of the incidental benefits of the ground keeper's post that he might sell-off the mown grass of the lawns for hay.

Very little is known about the social life of the pensioners, or about the way in which they occupied their leisure. There is no reason to suppose that they were very different from other members of the same social class. The only conspicuous additions to the recreational facilities of the almshouses were made in the second half of the nineteenth century. In 1872 Thomas Howard bequeathed a small annuity of about £16, for 'the provision of periodical and other publications for the amusement and instruction of the inhabitants of Sir Robert Geffrye's Almshouse'. The material accumulated in this way was supplemented by gifts from other members of the Company and eventually grew into a lending library, which was placed in the care of the matron. At the very end of the century, the new Victoria Room was built to provide a meeting place for the pensioners and the library was transferred into it. Among other furniture, the Victoria Room contained a piano and the last surviving resident told the Curator of the Museum in 1971 that the room was used for private entertainments, to which members of the Company often came as guests.

There is every indication that the almshouse routine was conducive to longevity. Perhaps it is not surprising that most of the pensioners lived to a good age in the reposeful surroundings of the almshouses. The full records of burials for the eighteenth century have not survived, but, between 1814 and 1850, the average age of death was between sixty-two and sixty-three. There were no marked fluctuations in the number of deaths per year during this period, despite the various epidemics of disease which broke out elsewhere in London, the usual number was between one and four. The greatest number of deaths occurred in 1839, when cholera was rampant, but all of the six who died were aged at least sixty-seven. The total number of burials in the almshouse ground in this period was roughly one hundred. The vast majority of pensioners' graves are unmarked by a headstone, the most conspicuous objects in the graveyard being the tombs of the two major benefactors, Sir Robert Geffrye and Thomas Betton.

The staff of the foundation

Small almshouses very often had no resident officer to look after the welfare of the inmates; at most a titular warden, charged with simple duties, like locking the doors at night, might be chosen from among the almspeople. Larger establishments, such as the Whittington Almshouses and Aske's and Trinity Hospitals, had a warden or chaplain. At the Geffrye Almshouses there was a strong emphasis on self-help and the pensioners were exhorted to be 'aiding and assisting to one another', but it was such a large foundation that a number of permanent officers were needed to look after their welfare and to undertake the maintenance of the fabric. The first officers were the chaplain and the ground keeper; to these were subsequently added the chapel clerk, the matron and the apothecary. The responsibilities of the various officers evolved into a well-organised system in the two-hundred years at Haggerston and a study of their duties provides much information about the changing nature of the almshouses.

Sir Robert had left no directions about the way in which his almshouses were to be staffed, but one of the stipulations of the Chancery Order of 1708 was that there should be a resident chaplain, with a salary paid out of the income of the Trust. For the first few years he probably received only the £10 a year allowed him out of Geffrye's Charity, possibly with an extra amount from the Company's own funds; this basic sum was later augmented by a number of private bequests. In 1719 William Chase left £10 yearly 'to a minister to read prayers daily and preach a sermon on Sundays at Geffrye's almshouses' and four years afterwards Thomas Betton left a further £10 for the same purpose. Both the company salary and the salary drawn from Geffrye's Charity were increased in the nineteenth century and by 1861 the chaplain received a total of £200 per year: £104 from the Company, £75 from Geffrye's charity, £10 each from Betton's and Chase's gifts, and a further £1 from Handson's gift.[28] At the same date most pensioners still only received £8 each from the Foundation and £10 each from Betton's gift.

The chaplain, who was the only officer not drawn from among the pensioners, was considered to be the representative of the Company in residence and *ex officio* warden of the foundation. This status was formally recognised in the printed rules hung up in the chapel. At first he was allowed two rooms in No 1 Staircase, which distinguished him from the pensioners who were only given one room. As we have seen, these rooms were furnished at the expense of the Company. While the chaplain was a single man two rooms were sufficient, but from the late eighteenth century onwards he was usually married and often had a large family. To allow for these larger establishments, the whole of No 1 Staircase was given over to the chaplain's use in 1793 and it continued as his official residence until the 1890s, when a non-resident chaplain was appointed who only required one room. The house was also fitted with a proper kitchen in one of the ground floor rooms and a water-closet in the basement. The railings in front of No 1, which still exist, were evidently intended as a mark of difference.

In the early years, the chaplains' duties seem to have been limited to the conducting of the regular religious observances and the burial services. The administration of the almshouse was undertaken almost entirely by the Committee and the chaplain was not, at first, a party to its decisions. His status gradually increased as the number of other officers grew and, by the 1870s, he had several supervisory tasks: he was to give the matron her instructions, to keep a general oversight of the library, to report any flagrant misbehaviour to the Committee and to submit to the Committee, twice yearly, a written report on the state of the almshouses. These duties do not sound very onerous but in an establishment as large as this there must have been a considerable amount of sick-bed visiting, especially in the later years when up to a quarter of the inhabitants at any one time were helpless and bed-ridden.

None of the chaplains was conspicuous in any direction. Most of them held their posts for long periods and conflicts over policy or ritual make no appearance in the records, with one exception. In September 1729, the Reverend Mr Scott was charged with 'ye following rudeness and misbehaviour, vizt, with throwing ye cushion over ye desk in ye presence of ye late master and severall other Gentlemen of ye Company after they had ordered it to be laid there, with refusing to read prayers when ye Master asked him to do so and with refusing to lett ye Master have ye key of ye buriall ground and sending him word by William Luttman, ye Beadle, to him and some other Gentlemen of ye Company that they were guilty of Sacrilege that he looked on them as no better than curs'd dogs.' The reason for this outburst is unknown, but Mr Scott was dismissed forthwith.

The ground keeper was the general factotum necessary in all institutions of any size. In May 1749 his duties were summarised as follows, 'Mowing the grass eight times a year carrying it off and rowling mending locks and latches within the house and new lining windows, looking after the clock, repairing the wharf at the backside the almshouses emptying the laystalls, emptying the boghouses, cutting the trees, rolling the walks and keeping them clean and clearing the ditch behind the almshouse'.[29] For this work he was paid £10 a year; the office was always filled by one of the pensioners and the salary was in addition to the annual pension of £6. From the 1770s, the ground keeper also served as chapel clerk, tolling the bell and keeping an attendance register, but at the end of the eighteenth century the jobs were separated, and remained so for over seventy years. However, by the time of the publication of a revised set of rules in 1886, they were once more combined. In the eighteenth century the ground keeper was just as likely to be a woman as a man; between 1750 and 1800 two women filled the post for a combined total of thirty-seven years. But, after a confrontation in 1787 with the owner of the land behind the almshouses, over the clearing-out of the drainage ditch, it was resolved not to employ any more women. There are no anecdotes to fill out the character of any of the ground keepers but one of them has the distinction of being the only known suicide in the history of the almshouses. He hanged himself in the chapel in the spring of 1887.

There was at first no housekeeper or matron at the almshouses, probably because the Committee were not enthusiastic about caring for the sick and preferred that they should be returned to their own parish. The first matron appointed seems to have been Rebecca Pugh, who is first mentioned in 1732. Like virtually all her successors she was chosen by the Committee out of the almshouse residents; only the last of the London matrons was brought in from outside. The great advantage of this arrangement was that the Charity did not have to provide a full salary, since part was already made up by the pension. In 1772 the matron was paid an allowance of £10, by 1835 she received a total of £42 and this had risen to £85 in 1892, of which £55 was salary and £30 pension.

Initially the work was more that of a housekeeper than a matron. It involved taking responsibility for all moveable items in the almshouses belonging to the Company, including the chapel linen and the plate, cutlery, tea and coffee requisite for the ceremonial breakfast at quarterly committee meetings. In addition, the housekeeper was to inspect the rooms of the inmates periodically and report any deterioration in their condition or any alteration which had not been sanctioned by the Committee. Over the years her responsibility for the welfare of the inmates steadily increased and ultimately became her principal function. Not only did she look after them and administer the treatment and drugs prescribed by the apothecary but she also kept the record of misdemeanors which was submitted to the chaplain. By the 1890s there were usually a small number of nurses resident in the rooms of the sicker inmates and these women also came under the supervision of the matron.

The Committee held its periodical meetings in one of the ground floor rooms of No 8 Staircase, adjacent to the chapel and, from the time of the first appointment, the matron was given rooms in the same staircase. At first she had only two rooms, but from 1820 she was allowed the whole of the staircase. The ground floor room, which had been enlarged in 1779, was kept as the Committee room, but the other three were her own. As in the case of the chaplain, the matron was given better facilities for cooking than the other pensioners.

Although the Trustees had anticipated the final requirements of the inmates by purchasing a burial ground, they seem to have been less concerned or sympathetic about their health. The rules exhorted all the inmates to aid and look after one another, but while this might be adequate for those who had become helpless, as a result of age, there was no satisfactory procedure for dealing with serious ailments or infectious diseases. From the committee minutes, it appears that, in the eighteenth century, unfortunate sufferers were removed from the almshouses and sent back to their parish of origin, presumably to die in the workhouse. This was the reason for insisting that each candidate for admission must have a certificate from their parish, agreeing to receive them back if they were expelled from the almshouse for any cause. Thus, on 23 June 1775, 'The Committee having been informed of the very bad state of health of Mrs Green, the Company's Porter and Rarus Jennings, one of Sir Robert Geffrye's pensioners, ordered that they be removed to their respective parishes'. Again, December 1781 'the committee were of the opinion that Anne Baker, one of the pensioners, should be removed from the almshouse on account of her being subject to fits'. In this instance, however, she was allowed to receive £6 a year as an out-pensioner.

Shortly after the removal of Anne Baker, the Committee became more sympathetic and, in 1795, recommended that any medical treatment necessary for the almspeople should be paid for out of the estate. This was followed shortly by the appointment of a permanent medical officer. An apothecary named John Weston, who had already treated some of the inmates, proposed an arrangement whereby he would attend any sick pensioners and supply any medicine necessary, for an annual fee of £12. His proposal was accepted in August 1802. Two years later the fee was increased to £25 and, in 1819, to £35 15s. Of the last sum, only £5 was drawn from the Geffrye estate and the remainder was given by the Company. Such further sums as were required to meet the cost of special treatment, or permanent attendance by a nurse, were also paid by the Company and not the Charity.

Increasing demands were made on this generosity in the nineteenth century, as the proportion of chronically infirm almspeople grew larger. By the end of the century, most of the rooms in the south wing were occupied by inmates who were bed-ridden and had to have their meals brought to them. For the last years of the almshouse in London the duties of the apothecary were discharged by one of the local doctors, who absorbed the almshouse into a general practice and held twice-weekly surgeries on the premises.

Chapter four

The end of the almshouses

The change in the character of Shoreditch in the nineteenth century

Many of the parishes on the east side of London were still more than half open land in 1800; Shoreditch, Bethnal Green and Stepney had not been developed to anything like the same extent as the northern or western edges of the City. The houses and other buildings were still clustered round the old village centres and along the main roads much as they had been in 1700. But by the middle of the nineteenth century all had changed: houses and factories had, in these fifty years, spread rapidly and remorselessly across the fields and gardens and covered them completely. The only unbuilt space was occupied by roads, canals and railways. The roads had always been there, but the traffic they carried steadily increased throughout the century. The Regent's Canal was built to connect the main commercial artery of the Grand Union Canal between London and Birmingham with the docks along the northern side of the Thames and opened in 1820. On either side of the new canal, factories sprang up to take advantage of the facilities which it offered and rows of small houses sprang up to accommodate the factory workers. As the docks spread further and further westward down the Thames, industry followed them and a belt of factories grew up along the north bank of the river.

In the late 1830s the railways arrived in London and it was not long before they spread over the eastern suburbs. All the major railway companies desired a line to the docks and, as the land here was relatively cheap, freight and marshalling yards were built by several companies very close to the docks whose trade they handled. Freight was of principal importance but passenger services were also brought into Fenchurch Street, into Broad Street and eventually to Liverpool Street. The North London Railway extension from Dalston Junction to Broad Street, which was opened on the 1 November 1865, must have been a matter of concern to many of the almspeople; the line was built for most of its length on a brick viaduct which ran close to the rear of the almshouses and completely screened the view towards the east. The only compensation was the provision of a station on the viaduct, immediately behind the main block of the almshouse. The building of the viaduct was the last stage in the encirclement of the Geffrye almshouses: the land on either side, fronting the Kingsland Road, had long been occupied by two other almshouses, Maria Street was laid out in the late 1820s, Elizabeth Place, on the north side, in the mid 1840s and Harriet Square, to the south, in 1864.[30] The opposite side of the Kingsland Road had been built up at least since 1800 and, by the 1820s, most of the land between here and Hoxton Street was covered with new streets. Many of the houses in these streets were built for the same respectable clerks and tradesmen who inhabited the new squares of Islington. The smaller houses, like those in Maria Street and Pearson Street to the east of Kingsland Road, were probably intended for better-off craftsmen. For a time, perhaps until the 1840s, the almspeople may have welcomed the increase in the number of houses for the consequent improvement in amenities, but henceforward the district around the almshouses became steadily less affluent and a less desirable place in which to live. The main reason for the change was probably the very rapid growth of the population. Besides the craftsmen and tradesmen, a substantial number of labourers and the very poor lived in the parish. As tenement houses in the centre of the City were demolished to make way for new banks and offices, more and more people of this kind removed to the parishes on the edge of London, especially those on the east side. Some of these immigrants were accommodated in new houses, but there was not room for all of them and soon houses in Shoreditch became crowded to overflowing. The building of railway lines across the parish, either to the docks or to the City termini, involved the demolition of large numbers of occupied houses and threw their inhabitants onto the streets. It was not until 1874 that it became usual for a re-housing clause to be inserted in every Act of Parliament for building a railway and not until the mid 1880s that this condition was enforced. The North London Railway extension, for example, displaced four thousand five hundred people between 1861 and 1864, most of whom remained in the parish.[31]

Overcrowding drove the more prosperous members of the community away from Haggerston and Hoxton to the suburbs, and they became the users of the railway which passed through the district in which they had formerly lived. By the 1860s, Shoreditch was among the poorest areas of London and the most densely populated; its houses were over-occupied and its inhabitants often unemployed or criminal. Policemen feared to venture down Hoxton High Street, or into the notorious 'Old Nichol' to the east of Shoreditch High Street. In the sea of small and overcrowded houses in the vicinity of the almshouses the only landmarks were the two great red-brick churches of St Columba's and St Chad's, built to the designs of James Brooks at the end of the 1860s, for the High-Church evangelising movement, and also the large parish workhouse next to St Columba's.

Such a drastic change in the condition of the parish was bound to have some effect on its many almshouses, whose occupants could no longer expect rest and quietness in this seething urban environment. The old people in the Geffrye almshouses were now seldom drawn from the local inhabitants and doubtless the same was true of several of the other almshouses. Many of these people had been born outside London and may very well have never lived in a town before their arrival in Shoreditch. The overcrowding of the area must have been disagreeable in itself but, in addition, the elderly were particularly vulnerable to the petty crimes of the district, purse-snatching and pocket-picking. For the various trustees, however, the decline in the character of the district was not wholly unfortunate. Many of the almshouses had been built on prime sites with a good frontage which were ideal for the building of warehouses or other commercial premises. The combined pressure from loss of amenity and increase of site value prompted many trustees to sell their land and buildings and move their pensioners to the country. The profits from the sale were usually enough to buy a new site, pay the cost of new and often more spacious buildings and leave sufficient capital in hand to increase the annual pensions and establish a maintenance fund. In some cases the whole idea of in-pensioners was abandoned and the proceeds of the sale were used to provide pensions for those living in their own homes, or were merged with another charity altogether. This alteration of charitable trusts was a national, not just a local phenomenon but because there were so many almshouses in Shoreditch the change there must have been striking. The pensioners at Watson's almshouses in Old Street were among the earliest to leave the parish when they removed to new buildings in Wanstead in 1859. Others soon followed suit: the Dutch Almshouses were displaced by the LNWR and removed to Charlton, Kent in 1865, the same year that most of the almshouses belonging to the parish itself were combined in one large establishment at Wood Green. The Haberdashers' Company discharged the inmates of their almshouses in Pitfield Street, rebuilt less than fifty years before, and converted the almshouse part of the charity to pensions. Of the row of three almshouses in the Kingsland Road, Harwar's, managed by the Drapers' Company, was the first to go and in 1879 the buildings were demolished and the charity converted to pensions. Strips of land on the west and south sides of the site were given up for road widening and the rest was let out for new building; seven new houses and shops were erected facing the Kingsland Road with a factory building at the south corner. The Framework Knitters' almshouses remained until 1906 but eventually moved for reasons which have already been related in Chapter Two; the site was then sold and Messrs Carwadine's premises built.

By contrast, the Trustees of the Geffrye Almshouses showed no signs of concern, either about the deteriorating character of Shoreditch or the steady removal of other almshouse foundations from the district. To some extent they could ignore the rest of Shoreditch; the large garden in front of the almshouse screened the buildings from the road outside and provided the almspeople with very adequate facilities for exercise and for taking the air. Neither was there any difficulty over the finances of the charity; the schemes of management had ensured a capital sum to pay for occasional repairs and it had also been possible to increase the pension in order to keep pace with the cost of living. In the early 1890s it became clear that some extensive repairs were necessary and the Trustees applied to the Charity Commissioners for permission to use a small amount of the accumulated repair fund; they wanted to install a new drainage system and to carry out other works to the interior and to the roof. But the Commissioners baulked at the quite moderate expense involved and instituted an enquiry into the condition of the almshouses. Although the report found the accommodation perfectly comfortable and habitable, the Commissioners were not convinced; a letter to the Secretary of the Company, written in January 1893, conveyed the information that, 'The Commissioners would, in the first place, suggest the desirability of selling the site of the present almshouse and reconstructing the charity in such a manner as to secure the necessary balance of income and expenditure.' To this the Company returned its architect's opinion that a modest outlay on improvements would make the building habitable for another fifty years. Matters dragged on until, in 1896, a sharp increase in Consols persuaded the Commissioners to agree to release the money for repairs.

To all appearance the Ironmongers were now firmly established in their refurbished buildings and determined to remain in Shoreditch until these had outlived their usefulness. This did not prevent covetous eyes being cast on the site and, most especially, on the garden which, by 1900, was one of the few remaining open spaces in the densely populated area. Shoreditch Vestry wrote to the Company in 1899 to ask if the Ironmongers' would consider selling the land; it was rumoured that the vestry had plans to build an electricity generating station on part of the site and use the rest as a recreation ground. This was, in fact, their intention and they petitioned the LCC to acquire the almshouses by compulsory purchase. At this point Mr Thackeray Turner, Secretary of the Society for the Protection of Ancient Buildings, wrote to the Company to ask if there was any chance that the site might be sold and he received the reply that, 'the Company do not propose to entertain any schemes which may involve the destruction of any part of the buildings or gardens belonging to the almshouses in Kingsland Road.' With this encouragement, the secretaries of both the SPAB and the National Trust wrote to the LCC urging that no hasty action should be taken; they also got up a petition against the removal of the almshouses. Their lobbying must have carried some weight and no further action was taken in the matter:[32] the generating station was finally built in Hoxton Square.

After this flurry of campaigning it seemed that the buildings were secure, since both the Company itself and the leading amenity societies were committed to their preservation and the higher powers of the Charity Commissioners and LCC were willing to concur. But only six years later the site of the Geffrye Almshouses was advertised for sale in *The Times*.[33]

The struggle over the preservation of the buildings

The Company's sudden change of heart must have been partly brought about by the belated realisation of the substantial profits to be made from the Kingsland Road site but, at first, the only reason publicly given for wishing to move the almshouses was the unsavoury nature of Shoreditch. In an explanatory letter to the Charity Commissioners, the Company Secretary claimed that 'the circumstances have destroyed all the amenities of the alms-houses and gardens and tend to preclude the inmates from the proper enjoy-ment of them, deterring them from going outside the gates or asking friends to visit them, and thus rendering the present site wholly unsuitable for the residence of persons who have been accustomed to a more or less refined life.' The Commissioners might well have asked what difference a mere ten years had made to the neighbourhood to make it so much less tolerable than it had been in the 1890s, if anything the LCC and other housing organisations had effected an improvement, but they did not raise this question. Perhaps the removal of the Framework Knitters' almshouses loomed large with the Ironmongers.

The advertisement in *The Times* alerted various amenity societies to the impending change and, in the six months following its appearance, a number of objections to the sale were received by the Charity Commissioners, who had to decide whether to give permission for the alteration of the trust. The SPAB and the National Trust wrote objecting to the demolition of the buildings and Shoreditch Vestry and the Metropolitan Public Gardens Association wrote to protest about the possible loss of open space. The Commissioners hesitated and meanwhile the Ironmongers pressed ahead with negotiations for the sale. In October 1907 the Company architects wrote to say that an offer of £24,000 for the site had been received from the Trustees of the Peabody Estate. If the sale was allowed, the almshouse site would be combined with the site of the houses on the west side of Maria Street, which had already been purchased by the Estate, to provide space for several new blocks of tenement dwellings to house a total of one thousand two hundred people. The Commissioners, who had so recently recommended the removal of the almshouses, still hesitated to give the necessary consent. The several petitions had made them aware of the interests opposed to the re-development of the site, which reflected a growing public opinion against the destruction of old buildings and green spaces solely on the grounds of financial gain. To resolve the problem, a local enquiry was announced, to be held on the 9 January 1908.

The transcript of the hearing is interesting, both for the information which it contains concerning the running of the almshouses and for the picture which emerges of this part of Shoreditch. The Company was represented by its officers, including the chaplain and the apothecary or medical officer. Opposing were the SPAB, the National Trust, the MPGA and the Borough. By an oversight, the LCC had not been formally requested by the Borough to appear, but unofficially it supported the opponents of the sale. Both the Master and Clerk of the Ironmongers stressed the cost of maintaining the old buildings and the lack of facilities available in them. The apothecary pointed out that the cellars were damp and unhealthy and that the noise of traffic passing along the Kingsland Road caused irritability and insomnia. The Surveyor made the best job he could of exposing the structural defects of a building which had been thoroughly repaired only a few years previously, comparing the almshouses, rather unfairly, with the dungeons at the Tower of London, as being very interesting but extremely undesirable to live in. The chaplain and the matron stressed the danger of robbery by the low class of people resident in the district. The matron was particularly vehement about the residents in Maria Street, whom she described as 'outcasts' and 'people of the lowest class' and accused them of throwing 'filth of the worst description' over the back wall. These officers were supported by the testimony of several of the alms-people, most of whom made great play of the filthy habits of their neighbours and the criminal character of the street.

In reply, the Vicar of St Columba's, across the road, defended the local population, denying that the inhabitants of Maria Street behaved any worse than those of other districts; the Vicar of Shoreditch pointed out that the inmates of the parish almshouses, which had recently moved out to Wood Green, complained constantly of the dreadful quiet in the country and of the difficulty of their friends coming to see them. Sir W Cremer, the local Member of Parliament and one of the JPs for the district, gave evidence in favour of retaining the open space and Edwin Lutyens, together with F W Troup who was consultant architect to the SPAB, expounded the architectural interest of the buildings and declared that they were in sound condition.

After two days of the enquiry had been spent in presenting the main outlines of the case both for and against removal, some more detailed information was produced. The Ironmongers announced that thirty-two inmates of the almshouse desired removal. Their opinions had been canvassed by Mrs Young, the matron, who remarked with satisfaction that those in favour of the move were 'full of loyalty to the Company.' But perhaps the most telling evidence was given by Dr Bryett, Medical Officer of Health for Shoreditch, who produced statistics to explain the condition of the district. In the whole Borough there were only seven acres of open space accessible to the public and more than half of this total was made up of church-yards and burial grounds. He pointed out that Shoreditch was the second most densely populated district in the whole of London; Haggerston, with a population density of one hundred and seventy-seven persons to the acre, was one of the better areas, but if the almshouses were replaced by Peabody dwellings the local density might equal Hoxton's fearful total of five hundred and forty-seven persons to the acre. Such an increase would certainly raise the death rate, which was already over twenty per thousand annually, again one of the highest in London.

In the summing-up the Counsel for the opponents of removal stressed the suddenness of the Company's change of heart, pointing out that until recently they had been firmly opposed to the idea, and suggested that the squalor of the area had been exaggerated in order to cover up the inconsistency. He pointed out that Geffrye's will had directed that the almshouses should be 'in or near London' and that a very strong case would be needed to justify removal. The Company's representative justified the desire to move the alms-house on financial grounds; the buildings were certainly not satisfactory but this alone would not have been a sufficient reason for the sale, and although the wishes of both the amenity societies and the Borough were applauded as worthy, they were rejected as unrealistic in financial terms.

Judgment was eagerly awaited by all parties, but especially by the amenity societies, because this was regarded by them as an important test case in the law affecting old and historic buildings. Two previous cases, both concerning almshouses in London, had produced differing results and the Geffrye Almshouses might decide the issue. In the earlier of these cases, heard in 1892, Mr Justice Chitty had refused to allow belated opposition to the sale and demolition of the Emmanuel Hospital in Buckingham Gate, Westminster. His ruling was an emphatic statement of the rights of private self-interest against intangible public benefits. After observing that one of the principal objects of the opponents of the sale was the preservation of the building 'on sentimental or aesthetic grounds' he went on to say that:

'A considerable portion of the letter or memorial of their (the objectors') solicitors submitting reasons against the sale is founded on such topics as the desirability of retaining open spaces in the metropolis and preserving ancient monuments or buildings—objects no doubt laudable in themselves, but all such topics have little or no relevancy upon the question now under consideration. Persons who entertain such opinions cannot ask that they should be enforced at the expense or to the detriment of others.'[34]

Four years later, the Brethren of Trinity House petitioned for leave to sell the site of the Trinity Almshouses in the Mile End Road and use the money for the payment of out-pensions, arguing that, by this means, a greater number of persons would enjoy the benefit of the charity. There was considerable opposition to the proposal from the cultural establishment of the day which was voiced in the national press. It was widely anticipated, on the basis of Mr Chitty's judgment, that the sale would be allowed, and one beneficial consequence was that C R Ashbee was impelled to produce a monograph on the building which was the first in the *Survey of London* Series, which is still continuing. In the event, the Charity Commissioners rejected the proposal, giving as their ground that there was no shortage of money and no other good reason why the bequest of Captain Mudd, who had given the land as well as the money for the building, should be tampered with. The decision followed a strict interpretation of the original bequest, but many of those whose principal object was the preservation of the buildings must have wondered if any weight had been given to their architectural merit. The Geffrye Almshouse enquiry was looked on to determine this question.

Assistant Commissioner Murray gave his judgment early in February 1908. After conceding that Haggerston was, in some respects not ideal as a situation for a resident charity, he pointedly observed 'it appears that the existing almshouses are not unsuitable for their purposes. No difficulty is experienced in finding inmates, the situation is not unhealthy, the almspeople live to a good old age.' Leaving aside the historic importance of the building and the value of the open space, he went on, 'the Trusts are for poor people, and though the trustees have been authorised to give a preference to the poor of the Ironmongers' Company there is otherwise no restriction as to any particular class. It appears to the Commissioners that such disadvantages as have been urged with regard to the situation of the Almshouses must be accentuated if the almspeople are chosen from among the class at present represented in many cases—the class, namely, of those who have been in a better position and have fallen into poverty. If, however, the almspeople were selected from the class presumably contemplated by the founder, that is to say, the London poor, the situation is not one to which objection would be made.' Murray considered that the case for sale had not been established and the Ironmongers' were refused leave to dispose of the almshouses. In announcing this decision the Charity Commissioners stated that they were not precluded from taking into consideration the question of public policy which had been indicated by Parliament with regard to the desirability of retaining open spaces in London and of preserving ancient buildings. The amenity societies were extremely pleased with this decision, which upheld their position, but the case was by no means concluded.

Almost immediately, the Ironmongers applied for leave to appeal to the Court of Chancery, which could not be denied since, technically, they were appealing under the suit begun against Sir Gabriel Roberts in 1707 and still pending. The appeal was heard in June 1909. Affidavits were taken from the officers of the Company, but the hearing was in chambers and the opponents of the sale were not allowed to be heard. The only fresh evidence came from the architect W D Caroë who had surveyed the almshouses for the Attorney General. His findings must have discomfited the Ironmongers; he had found no evidence of foundational settlement or any other serious decay and declared at the end of his report, 'Architecturally, I consider that these Alms-houses are an object lesson as to how such buildings should be dealt with. It would be difficult to better them. I have little doubt that when erected they were regarded as among the best of their class.'[35] But in the end it was Mr Chitty's judgment which carried the day and, on 12 March 1910, *The Times* reported the hearing with the information that the appeal had been successful.

How the almshouses became a museum

There was no more to be hoped from the Company, which hastened to complete the sale of the site to the Peabody Trust. All those interested in the preservation of buildings or gardens now turned to the LCC as a last resort. Even though the Council had not been represented at the Charity Commission hearing, many of its elected members had followed the proceedings with keen interest. The Local Government and Records Committee was anxious that the buildings should be retained, the Parks Committee had a covetous eye on the garden and the Public Health Committee was concerned with the threat to the lawns and trees which constituted fourteen per cent of the useable open space in the Borough. Encouraged by letters from the SPAB, National Trust, MPGA, and Shoreditch Borough Council, as well as by a petition from some of the local inhabitants, these Committees decided to press for the acquisition of the whole site by the Council.

By the London County Council (General Powers) Act of 1898 the Council had acquired the authority to purchase 'by agreement' buildings and places of architectural or historic interest; similar powers over gardens were given by the Open Spaces Act of 1906. On this occasion, it was probably the value of the site as open space which carried greater weight, but the end result was satisfactory to all parties. Following two detailed reports from the Local Government and the Parks Committee, the full Council agreed on 10 May 1910 that the sum of £16,000 would be contributed towards the purchase of the site, the remainder to be raised by the Borough, or by public subscription. At the end of the year the Council agreed to purchase the houses on the east side of Maria Street from the Peabody Trustees for a further sum of £10,000. In the event, the Borough was unable to raise the required money from the rates and was forced to borrow £6,000 from the LCC, to be repaid over fifty years; the remaining £2,000 was raised by subscription within the borough. The purchase of both pieces of land was completed on 6 December 1911. The Ironmongers had not been prepared to wait while the various bureaucratic procedures were carried through, but the Peabody Trustees magnanimously agreed to buy the almshouses from the Company and re-sell to the LCC at the same price. By this sale, the LCC became the owner of the almshouses and garden and Nos 21-61 (odd) Maria Street. Four-fifths of the purchase price was taken from the budget of the Parks Committee and only one fifth from that of the Local Government Committee, a clear indication of the relatively greater importance of the garden to the LCC. The new open space was opened to the public only a week after it had been acquired without any improvements having been carried out. Nevertheless, it was felt necessary to re-organise the layout of the garden and also to demolish the Maria Street houses in order to turn the land between the almshouses and the street into a children's playground with a gravelled surface. These works were completed in six months and the gardens were formally opened on 27 July 1912. But the problem of how the buildings should be used remained to be solved.

During the negotiations for the sale, the possible uses of the almshouse building were hardly considered. The Parks Committee, anxious to maximise space, suggested that both wings should be demolished leaving only the central block. This proposal was resisted by the Local Government Committee, whose members were anxious to keep all the buildings standing: they felt that they might be converted to provide extra housing for the area, but the matter was not decided. By coincidence, a petition had been presented to the Council early in 1911, requesting that 'a Central Museum and Exhibition Room' should be established where the work of young craftsmen, who had been trained in the Council's own technical and craft schools might be displayed. The petition declared that 'A permanently open exhibition is requisite—wide enough in its scope to serve as a Record Office, and contributions from which could be sent to different localities requiring such examples—where the student can examine what has been done by his compeers, can learn what has been shown, by competent selection, to be a fine standard of technical and artistic excellence, to which he can go for the same educational advantage to himself as can be obtained—so far as work in the past is concerned—at the Victoria and Albert Museum in South Kensington.' The petition was signed by 'persons especially interested in the Education of Craftsmen in the various art industries of the Country'; these included Halsey Ricardo, Master of the Art Workers' Guild, Omar Ramsden, Harry Redfern, William de Morgan, Edwin Lutyens, Sidney Webb, Aston Webb, Sir Lawrence Alma-Tadema, Richard Norman Shaw, George Frampton, Walter Crane and E S Prior and most of the leading members of the creative establishment[36]. One surprising omission from the list was W R Lethaby, Principal of the Central School of Arts and Crafts and the leading figure in craft education at this time; possibly his position as an employee of the LCC forbade him to take part.

The petition was referred to the Local Government Committee, which seized on it as a possible solution to the problem of finding a use for the buildings of the Geffrye Almshouses. The Committee rejected the idea of having one large respository for all the arts and crafts, but suggested instead that there should be a number of smaller museums, set up in various districts of London, wherever a particular trade was strongest. Many of the craft industries in London were still localised at this date, to an extent which made the suggestion more reasonable than it seems today, if more parochial than the national centre proposed in the petition. The following centres of industry were instanced by the Committee in support of their own proposals: Lambeth for pottery, Shoreditch for furniture making, Finsbury and Southwark for printing, paper and stationery, Spitalfields for the remaining fragments of the silk weaving industry, Bethnal Green for bootmaking, Hatton Garden for diamond cutting, Clerkenwell for watchmaking, Bermondsey for leather dressing, South West London for the building trades, South East London for engineering and Whitechapel for cigars. In their report to the Council, the members of the Committee declared 'in London the principle of special industrial museums in suitable centres is the right one upon which to proceed' and they suggested that the Geffrye Almshouses might be converted to serve as the first of such centres, with a permanent display of woodwork and furniture of various periods and also a changing collection of modern work to advertise the skills of living craftsmen. The older work would provide high quality examples for young craftsmen and apprentices to follow and these practical examples would be backed up by a library on the subject of woodworking, housed in the Victoria Room which had previously served the almspeople as a library. To strengthen the appeal of the proposal, the Committee reported that the Victoria and Albert Museum had been approached and would be willing to lend a certain amount of period furniture and it was anticipated that local industries would be glad to lend examples of their current work for display.

This was a far-seeing idea, anticipating by half a century the prominence now given to local crafts and other aspects of daily life in museums all over the country and it is greatly to the credit of the LCC that it was accepted.

On the 18 December 1912, the Council agreed to sanction the conversion of the buildings for use as a museum, according to the scheme which had already been proposed by the Architect's Department. In order to minimise cost it was decided that only the main range should be converted at first. The physical effects of this conversion have been discussed in Chapter 2 Part 3. The works were begun in February 1913 and were virtually completed by May of the same year. The central block was opened to the public on 2 January 1914 under the name of the Geffrye Museum. The fortunes of the buildings from this time forward have already been related and the evolution of the Museum's collection, though fascinating, is dealt with in a number of other publications and is not a matter for this book.

Postscript—The Ironmongers' almshouses at Mottingham and Hook.

The location chosen by the Ironmongers for their new almshouses was Mottingham, near Bromley in Kent. A large site was purchased next to the Mottingham Road and five acres of it was set aside for the almshouse buildings and gardens. Although the number of pensioners was not increased, more accommodation was provided for each one and the buildings were therefore considerably more extensive than those in Shoreditch.

The new buildings were designed by George Hubbard, the Surveyor to the Company, in the style of the early eighteenth century. Wrought iron gates on the main road lead directly to a large central pavilion with a pedimented front nine bays wide and an ornamental doorcase. On either side are long two-storey wings, each with three entrances with finely-carved wooden doorcases. Short rear wings of similar appearance extend at right angles to the main ranges. All the buildings are of red brick, with stone ornaments and wooden modillion cornices. A separate chapel, in a simplified version of the same style, was added behind the main block in 1934 to the design of Sydney Tatchell.

Under the name of 'Geffrye's Homes' these buildings served the purposes of the Charity for sixty years. During the Second World War, however, the south wing was damaged in an air raid and left a ruin. Shortly after the war had ended the Company decided to move the almshouses away from London altogether and in 1974 new buildings, designed by Evan, Roberts & Partners, were erected at Hook in Hampshire. The new homes incorporated a number of items from earlier buildings particularly associated with the Company, among which was the lead statue of Sir Robert which had been made by Van Nost for the original almshouses and which now stands at the entrance to the new homes. The Mottingham buildings, like their predecessors in Shoreditch, were acquired by the Greater London Council and are still used to provide accommodation for the elderly.

Footnotes

1   Several wills of the Geffrye family are listed among those proved in the Consistory Court of the Bishop of Exeter (Index Library, Vol 46). The originals were destroyed in the last war.

2   Index of Freemen of the Ironmongers' Company (Guildhall Ms 16,978) Volume 1, 36.

3   William Foster *The East India House,* 1924
It appears, from a plan reproduced on page 146, that Geffrye's house stood on the west side of Lime Street, immediately north of Leadenhall Place.

4   W K Jordan *Philanthropy in England,* 1959, 241.

5   *Ibid.*

6   David Owen *English Philanthropy 1660-1960,* 1965, Chapter 3.

7   PRO, PCC Wills 1704 Ashe Volume 63 (Prob 11/475).

8   PRO, C9/332/55 (Executor's Accounts.)

9   The minutes of this committee (Guildhall Ms 17,052) form the principal source of information about the building and administration of the almshouses. After 1722 the committee minutes were incorporated in the Court Books (Ms 17,080).

10   PRO, C9/332/55: C10/380/14

11   Company Letter Book (Guildhall Ms 17,080), Volume 2.

12   MLR 1712, Volume 5.

13   Daniel Defoe *A Tour Through London About The Year 1725*

14   Commons' Journals, 29 April 1712.

15   'Castle glass' was another name for the common glass used in less important buildings. See, for example, Isaac Ware, *'Compleat Body of Architecture'* Bk X Chapter II, 742 and 748.

16   Wren Society Volume IV, 34.

17   The information about Burford's Bedford Row speculation was contributed by Mr A F Kelsall of the GLC Historic Buildings Division.

18   PRO, PCC Wills 1725, Brook fol 72.

19   The Drapers' Almshouses in Priscilla Road, Poplar and the now demolished Emmanuel Almshouses in Buckingham Gate, Westminster are two examples of almshouses with a pedimented centre which pre-date the Geffrye almshouses.

20   MLR 1716, Volume 1/4.

21   Details of these bequests are given in Mr Hare's report on the Ironmongers' Company charities, contained in the Report of Her Majesty's Commission to Enquire into Livery Companies of the City of London (1884), Volume IV, 517 ff.

22   One of the downstairs rooms in staircase No 13 had a fitted dresser across the whole width of the rear wall. This was removed in the 1950s.

23   'An Account of the Receipts and Payments of the Worshipful Company of Ironmongers touching the Charity of Sir Robert Geffryes Deceased' (Guildhall Ms 17,056/1).

24   Charity Commissioners, File 219153 A/4.

25   *Notes and Queries* Series 10, Volume VI, 264.

26   Robert Seymour *A Survey of the Cittyes of London and Westminster, etc,* 1734/5, 220-222.

27   There are two later sets of rules in the Guildhall Library, dating from 1873 and 1886.

28   For details of these bequests see Mr Hare's report (note 21 above).

29   Ironmongers' Company Court Books (Guildhall Mss 16, 967), Volume 10, 2 May 1749.

30   These are the dates at which the various streets first appear in the parish rate books.

31   H P White *A History of the Railways of Great Britain*, Volume III (Greater London), 73.

32   Information from the file on the almshouses preserved at the Society for the Protection of Ancient Buildings.

33   *The Times* 4 August 1906 16.

34   *The Times* 6 July 1892 contains a report of the proceedings.

35   Charity Commissioners file 219153 A/4.

36   The full list of the signatories to the petition is as follows:

Lord Argyll, Halsey Ricardo, F W Troup, R le B Rathbone, H Massé, Omar Ramsden, Harold Stabler, Emery Walker, Harry Redfern, Harry Napper, Graley Hewitt, S A Vaneto, Thomas Okey, Hubert French, Selwyn Image, Lord Weardale, Lord Lytton, J Lockwood Kipling, William de Morgan, Sidney Colvin, G W Prothero, Edwin Lutyens, G Baldwin Brown, Lord Balcarres, Sidney Webb, the Earl of Carlisle, W H Godfrey, P Geddes, F C Mears, F J Cobden-Sanderson, W A S Benson, J L Myers, W B Richmond, C H Reilly, Georgiana Burne-Jones, (illegible), Aston Webb, Luke Fildes, Alfred East, M H Spielman, Frank Dicksee, J W Waterhouse, L Alma-Tadema, Andrew Gow, R Norman Shaw, Hamo Thorneycroft, Ernest Waterlow, Seymour Lucas, Henry Pegram, Ernest Crofts, Ernest George, Charles Sims, George Frampton, M R Colton, Leonard Stokes, Walter Crane, E S Prior, (illegible), May Morris, Thackeray Turner, Stirling Lee.

Abbreviations used in the footnotes

MLR   Middlesex Land Register in Greater London Record Office, County Hall, SE1.

PRO   Public Record Office.

Appendix one

The original rules of the almshouses

Rules to be observed by the inmates of Sir Robert Geffrye's almshouses

Imprimis: It is ordered that, upon the death of any person, that is, or shall be chose into the said almshouse, to partake of the said charity, there shall be at the next quarterly court, after the death of the said person, another person chose in the room of the said person so deceased.

II That any relation of the said benefactor that is a proper object shall be preferred to any other petitioner; And in defect of any such relation petitioning, it is ordered that any member or their widow that have been Liverymen or Freemen of the Company of Ironmongers, who is a proper object, shall be preferred to any other petitioner: but in defect of any such petitioning, the greatest object that shall petition shall be chosen without favour or affection.

III That such person be chose in for his, or her life, he or she obeying and fulfilling all the following orders, but be liable to be expelled upon being guilty of such crimes as are hereafter mentioned, to be punished with expulsion.

IV That it be a general rule to be observed that no person to be chose under fifty-six years of age (not to be dispensed with) unless upon some extraordinary occasion.

V That no person chose shall have the use and benefit of more than one room and partition in the cellar, which shall be assigned them by the wardens.

VI That if any person chose be a married man, it may be lawful for his wife to cohabit with him, she observing and obeying all these orders; but upon her husband's decease his widow is to relinquish the almshouse, unless being qualified by her age, she shall be elected herself.

VII That the honour and service of Almighty God being above all things to be respected, it is ordered that all abiding in the almshouse, men and women being in health, and well able to walk, shall every Lord's day, and days of public fast, or thanksgiving, in the year, go either to their parish church, or some other place where divine service to Almighty God is performed, and to abide there to hear, attend and perform Divine Worship; and for neglect thereof shall forfeit 4d for every offence, to be deducted out of the next payment of their pensions.

VIII That if any of the said almspeople shall use any blasphemous words, tending to the dishonour of Almighty God, he or she, for the first offences shall forfeit 6d, for the second offence 1s and for the third offence, shall be expelled the almshouse for ever.

IX That if any of the said almspeople shall commit adultery, fornication, or any such like uncleaness, or shall steal within the house or without, or usually beg in any place without the house, or shall frequent any house or houses suspected of lewdness, or admit or receive commonly to his or her room, such person or persons, which are, or have been, infamous for lewd lives, he or she so offending, and being duly proved, shall be expelled the almshouse for ever.

X That if any of the said almspeople shall at any time, or times, either within the house or without, be drunk, he or she so offending (besides the penalty of the law in this behalf provided) shall, for the first offence forfeit 4d, for the second 8d, for the third 1s 4d and for the fourth shall be expelled the house for ever.

XI That none of the almspeople shall give any railing, bitter or un-charitable speeches, or give any stripes or blows, to any of their fellows, upon forfeiture of a month's pay for the first offence and expulsion for the second.

XII That none but such as are of good life and conversation, certified by certificates signed by known and reputable persons, swearers, known adulterers, or fornicators, no thief, common drunkards, scolds, or unquiet person or persons, shall be elected or continued in the said almshouse.

XIII That if any of the said almspeople shall lye out of the same by night without license of the Master, or one of the wardens, or some lawful excuse to be approved of by them, for the first offence shall forfeit out of their pay 4d for the second offence double, or repeating the same offence above three times in one year shall be expelled.

XIV That none of the said almspeople shall harbour or lodge any stranger, young child, or children, in his, or her chamber; nor take any woman to attend him or her, but in time of sickness only, and no other but his or her sister, daughter, or some near relation, or some woman of good conversation, not under fifty years of age, on pain to lose or forfeit, for every night any person be harboured, or lodged, contrary to this order, 5s, to be stopped out of their pension.

XV That none of the poor of the said almshouse shall make any alteration in their room, under colour, to amend their lodging on any pretence what-soever, without direction of the Master or Wardens, upon pain of expulsion.

XVI That none of the almspeople shall spoil or break down any walls or fences, or trees planted, or to be planted, upon penalty to forfeit 1s besides to make good the same at their own charge.

XVII That none of the said almspeople shall cast, or lay any rubbish dust, or any noisome thing whatsoever, within any part of the said almshouse, or any ditch adjoining thereto, or any the walks, or passages thereof, to the annoyance of any of their fellows, but shall keep their rooms and the walks, ways and passages before their doors, sweet and clean, or for every offence herein to forfeit 4d.

XVIII That none of the almspeople shall sell, or vend, any strong beer, ale, brandy, spirits or other liquors, either publicly, or privately, upon pain of expulsion.

XIX That none of the said almspeople shall teach, school or exercise any trade, or occupation, that may be prejudicial, or dangerous to the building or annoyance, or disturbance to their fellows, or that shall require the assistance of any other person, on forfeiture of 12d per week, so long as they transgress.

XX That all persons belonging to the said almshouses, shall return, and come to their said several lodgings (except licensed by the Master or one of the Wardens, to be absent for some short time) between the first day of October, to the first day of March yearly, at, or before, the hour of seven o'clock in the evening, of those days; and between the first day of March and the first day of October, yearly, at, or before, the hour of nine o'clock, upon forfeit of 4d for the first offence; for the second 8d, for the third 12d and for the fourth to be expelled.

XXI That once every quarter, all the offences that are punishable by forfeitures, shall be heard and decided, and fined by the Master, or one of the Wardens of the Company of Ironmongers; assisted by any three of more of the Livery, in hearing of as many of the almspeople as can be got together for example sake.

XXII That all the offences aforesaid, that are punishable by expulsion, shall be heard and judged by the Master, Wardens and Livery, in a general court assembled at their Hall; and whosoever, by the majority of the said court, shall be ordered to be expelled, shall never after be capable to be chose again, or be admitted into the said almshouse; but a padlock shall be put upon their door, and their goods delivered to them, or placed in the cellar under the great room, till they fetch them away; and any of the said almspeople that shall lodge them afterwards in their chamber, shall forfeit 12d for every night they shall entertain them.

XXIII That if any the said almspeople die, their gowns shall be for the benefit of such person as shall be chose in their room, upon penalty of losing what pension shall be due at the time of their decease.

XXIV That if any of the said almspeople die, the charge of their burial shall be defrayed by their friends and relations, before they move their goods.

XXV That none of the almspeople shall refuse to be aiding and assisting to one another; and in case of sickness, 'tis expected they shall, by turns, attend, assist, and be helpful to each other; and live in peace and unity one with another: and which of them shall refuse their good offices to another in sickness, shall, upon good proof, be expelled the house.

XXVI That a proper person shall be appointed by the said company at a court, to keep the key of the gates from time to time, at their pleasure; who shall be required to give a just and impartial account of all offences committed against any of the orders herein contained.

XXVII That the forfeitures be divided into three parts; one to the informer, the other two parts to be put into a common box, and be divided every Christmas among the poor of the said almshouse, at the discretion at the Master and Wardens or any two of them.

XXVIII That these orders, being fairly printed, shall be hung up in the great room, and read publicly there, in the presence of the almspeople, twice in the year, viz, on, or near, the 25 March and 29 September; and that another copy be kept by the Clerk of the Ironmongers' Company, to have recourse to on occasion.

XXIX That such further orders as the Company shall make, shall be binding.

Appendix two

Other almshouses in Shoreditch

Other almshouse foundations within the parish of Shoreditch

Aldermanbury Almshouses, Philip Street, Hoxton

These four almshouses are marked on Stanford's map of 1868. There is no known documentation for them, but a tablet which used to be on one of them stated that they were the property of Mr Malcott, and were built in 1817.

Aske's Hospital, Pitfield Street

Robert Aske, by will dated January 1689, left £20,000 to the Haberdashers' Company to establish an almshouse for twenty poor single freemen and a school for twenty sons of freemen. The charity was settled by Act of Parliament in 1690 and the site in Pitfield Street bought. The first buildings, designed by Robert Hooke, were erected in 1695. In 1822 these were demolished and replaced in 1825-27 by buildings designed by David Riddel Roper, which increased the extent of the school. In 1873 the Charity Commissioners approved a scheme which converted the almshouse part of the charity to pensions and much extended the educational provisions; the almshouse parts of the buildings were demolished and the schools again enlarged. In 1898 the schools were removed and the premises taken by the London County Council as the Shoreditch Technical Institute; they now form part of the City and East London College.

Badger's Almshouse, Hoxton Street

Allen Badger, by will of 1674, left property in Norton Folgate to Shoreditch Parish, the rents to accumulate until there was sufficient money to build six almshouses. In 1698 the fund was used to buy land on the east side of Hoxton Street, just north of Old Street; the land was bought from Daniel Badger. Allen Badger had asked that the six beneficiaries be men of the parish, but in the event women were always appointed. In 1873 a proposal to move the almshouses to Tottenham, with other foundations, was not acted upon, the almshouses were demolished and the fund merged with other charities and converted to pensions.

Berman's Almshouses, Hoxton Street and Basing Square

William Berman of Hoxton set up the almshouse trust by his will, dated in 1700 and proved in 1703. His executors acquired a site just to the east of Hoxton Street and erected the almshouses. Early in the nineteenth century, probably in 1813, new almshouses were built a little to the east in Basing Square, just off the Kingsland Road. Both sets of almshouses have disappeared. Berman was a presbyterian minster and the foundation was for eight women, but it is not known whether the foundation was denominational. The almshouses were sometimes referred to as Baremere's Almshouses or Bernander's Almshouses.

Bourne's Almshouses, Kingsland Road

Thomas Bourne, by will of 1727, left money for the building and maintenance of almshouses for twelve freemen of the Framework Knitters' Company. Management of the almshouses was placed with the Company. In 1734 a site was acquired on the east side of the Kingsland Road and the almshouses built. In 1907 the foundation moved to Oadby, Leicestershire, and the Shoreditch almshouses were demolished.

Dutch Almshouses, Whitecross Alley

The Dutch Church in London had some sort of poor house by 1562. In 1685 a lease was taken, and in 1688 the freehold bought, of a site on which the almshouses were built at the cost of the church. The trustees were the elders of the church and the beneficiaries fifteen poor members of the Dutch Church in Austin Friars; in 1714 it was said that 26 poor were housed there. Two of the almshouses were endowed by Egbert Guede in 1727. The site lay between Crown Street (now Sun Street) Shoreditch and Whitecross Alley, by Mulberry Court. In 1865 this site was taken by the London and North Western Railway and the foundation moved to Charlton, Kent.

Fuller's Hospital, Old Street

John Fuller, a judge and sometime Treasurer of the Inner Temple, by will of 1592 directed his widow and heirs to build two almshouses, one for twelve men in Stepney the other for twelve women in Shoreditch; the governors were intended to be the Mercers' Company. The Shoreditch almshouses were built before 1605 by Fuller's widow, who added an endowment on her death in 1623. The site was on the south side of Old Street. The foundation was not incorporated as Fuller had intended until 1680, when it was said that the beneficiaries were a warden and eleven others, all single women aged over 50. The management, however, was vested in the parish, not in the Mercers' Company or the incorporated body. The almshouses were rebuilt in 1787 and demolished in 1865 when the foundation moved to Wood Green.

Fuller's Almshouses, Hoxton Street

Six almshouses were established in 1794 by a Mr Fuller for twelve women of Presbyterian denomination. They were situated on the west side of Hoxton Street by George Square.

Hackney Road Almshouses

A site in Hackney Road has been bought by the parish of Shoreditch in 1625 for a burial ground. In 1825 an engine-house and watch-house were built there, and this building was converted into the almshouses in 1833. The beneficiaries were three, later four, old men of the parish, two of whom had previously been employed as keepers of the parish watch-houses. No trust was established and the parish maintained the almshouses out of miscellaneous unappropriated charity income. The building was demolished in 1904 when the foundation moved to St Leonard's House, part of the united parish almshouses at Wood Green.

Harwar's Almshouses, Kingsland Road

Samuel Harwar bequeathed money in 1704 to be used by his executors in building almshouses similar to those given by Mr Pemel to the Drapers' Company. The beneficiaries were to be three freemen and three widows of freemen of the Company, and three men and three widows of the parish in which the almshouses were built. The management of the almshouses was entrusted to the Company. A site was taken on the east side of Kingsland Road and almshouses built in 1713. In 1879 the buildings were demolished and the charity was converted to pensions.

Hillier's Almshouses, Curtain Street

Founded in 1800 for seven poor women, one of whom was to be of the Rev Reynold's dissenting congregation in Camomile Street, one of whose deacons was always to be a trustee. The Camomile Street congregation later merged with the City Temple.

Lady Lumley's Almshouse, Shepherdess Walk

Elizabeth, Viscountess Lumley, established a trust in 1657 for building eighteen almshouses, twelve in Thornton Dale, Yorkshire and six in either St Botolph, Aldgate or St Botolph, Bishopsgate, the latter to be for the benefit of three poor from each parish. The parochial authorities were trustees for their respective shares. In 1672, after failing to find a site in the named parishes, the trustees were authorised by the Lord Chancellor to use part of the Underwood charity land in Shoreditch belonging to Bishopsgate parish to build the six almshouses for which they had contracted with a carpenter. The site was on the east of Shepherdess Walk at its southern end. The almshouses were repaired in 1781 and rebuilt in 1822. In 1891 the Bishopsgate half was merged into the Bishopsgate Foundation, which in 1897 bought out the Aldgate half of the almshouses premises, the money being merged with the Aldgate Freedom and Lordship Foundations. In 1898 the almshouses were demolished when the Bishopsgate Foundation let the site for building, and the funds have since been used for general charitable purposes.

Morrell's Almshouses, Goldsmith's Row

Richard Morrell, by will of 1703, bequeathed money for the erection of six almshouses for poor members of the Goldsmiths' Company, which was entrusted with their management. The almshouses were built in 1705; they were reported old and in need of repair in 1863 and were presumably demolished soon after this.

Old Gloucester Street Almshouses

Four almshouses in Old Gloucester Street (now Crondall Street) were built circa 1800 on ground given to the parish of Shoreditch in 1596. They were described as the Old Gloucester Street Almshouses by John Ware in 1836, and would seem to be those, or on the site of those, marked on Stanford's map of 1868 as 'Fuller's Almshouses'.

Shoreditch New Almshouses, Kent Street

In 1847 a committee was formed and subscription opened for a fund to build almshouses for poor women of the parish of Shoreditch. Ground was purchased in Kent Street, Haggerston, and almshouses to accommodate twenty people built in 1852. They were designed by Mr T E Knightly. The buildings were demolished after the last war.

Walter's and Porter's Almshouses, Old Street

Money for eight almshouses was left by John Walter, clerk to the Drapers' Company, by will of 1656. A site on the north side of Old Street was acquired and the almshouses built by 1658 when they were endowed by Walter's widow, Alice Walter, and placed under the management of the Drapers' Company. The Company appointed two almspeople, Shoreditch parish the other six. An additional eight almshouses were given to the parish by Thomas Porter in 1826, when the foundation took their joint names. The same site was used for the rebuilding of the original eight almshouses and the new eight, which were designed by a Mr (probably John) Wallen. The foundation moved to Wood

Green in 1902 and is now administered by Shoreditch United Charities, the Drapers' Company having severed its connections with the trust.

Watson's Almshouses, Old Street

William Watson was the leading contributor to the cost of almshouses built in 1670 by the Weavers' Company for the widows of 12 poor freemen of the Company. They were Company almshouses not subject to a specific trust. A site on the north side of Old Street was leased by the Company for 200 years from 1668. The almshouses, built in 1670, were rebuilt in 1824 at the cost of C J Coverly, a member of the Court of the Company. As the end of the lease approached, and the Company's mens' almshouses in Spitalfields were taken for the widening of Commercial Street, the Company resolved to move both establishments to new premises at Wanstead, which move took place in 1859.

Westby's Almshouses, Pitfield Street

Ten almshouses were built by Mrs Mary Westby and her sister Mrs Bromsdale in 1749 and an endowment was provided in 1750. The beneficiaries were widows or spinsters who were to be protestant dissenters, 'professing the Presbyterian, Independant or Antipaedobaptist tenets'. The almshouses were colloquially known as the 'Old Maids' Almshouses', especially after 1749 when it was determined that at least two of the beneficiaries were to be unmarried. The trustees were drawn from three dissenting congregations in the City. The site was acquired and almshouses built in Hoxton Causeway in 1749. The premises were sold to the School Board for London in 1881 when the buildings were demolished and the charity converted to a pensions charity.

Designed by GLC Supplies Department (Printing and Graphic Design Division) and printed by Heffers Printers Limited Cambridge 24283 2/79